The Unofficial Guide to Building Your Business in the

Second Life®
Virtual World

D1529741

The Unofficial Guide to Building Your Business in the

Second Life®
Virtual World

Marketing and Selling Your Product,
Services, and Brand In-World

Sue Martin Mahar
and Jay Mahar

AMACOM

American Management Association

New York • Atlanta • Brussels • Chicago • Mexico City • San Francisco
Shanghai • Tokyo • Toronto • Washington, D.C.

Special discounts on bulk quantities of AMACOM books are available to corporations, professional associations, and other organizations. For details, contact Special Sales Department, AMACOM, a division of American Management Association, 1601 Broadway, New York, NY 10019.
Tel.: 212-903-8316.   Fax: 212-903-8083.
Website: www.amacombooks.org

This publication is designed to provide accurate and authoritative information in regard to the subject matter covered. It is sold with the understanding that the publisher is not engaged in rendering legal, accounting, or other professional service. If legal advice or other expert assistance is required, the services of a competent professional person should be sought.

Library of Congress Cataloging-in-Publication Data

Mahar, Sue Martin.
    The unofficial guide to building your business in the Second Life® virtual world : marketing and selling your product, services, and brand in-world / Sue Martin Mahar And Jay Mahar.
        p.   cm.
    Includes bibliographical references and index.
    ISBN-13: 978-0-8144-1270-1
    ISBN-10: 0-8144-1270-X
        1. Second Life® (Web site)   2. Shared virtual environments—Economic aspects.   3. Internet industry.
    4. Internet marketing.   5. Electronic commerce.   I. Mahar, Jay.   II. Title.

    HD9696.8.U64S436   2009
    658.8—dc22
                                                                                2008035794

Printing number

10 9 8 7 6 5 4 3 2 1

This collaborative work is dedicated to our children,
and to all of "Generation I"

Contents

Acknowledgments

Leading the way down an unknown path takes a measure of good instinct, intelligence, and a sense of adventure, especially if that path is a virtual one. Entering into Second Life® while it was virtually unknown has been an exciting adventure and a life lesson.

We would like to acknowledge several people who have been part of our life's lesson, real and virtual. We would also like to thank those who have shared our enthusiasm, and cleared the path for us to share with the world what we have learned.

Without Jay's knowledge and craftsmanship ability with technology and the market, I would not be writing these words, nor would I have the friends and opportunities I have through the virtual world. I would not have been able to create a life like this on my own. Although I still would be writing, it would not likely be on this fantastic subject. Thank you.

We both have our parents to thank. Their love and support has carried us through tough times. They are from "The Greatest Generation," aptly named. Though they may not fully understand the span of the Metaverse, which is forming for future generations, they are proud of us for participating in something on such a grand scale. Our valiant mothers share the pride of this book enough for all our 11 siblings and their spouses, 26 nieces and nephews, and our fathers, who rest in heaven.

We spoke with several industry leaders at IBM®, such as Dr. Colin Parris, Vice President of Digital Convergence, and Grady Booch, respected IBM® Fellow and author of several software books. David Lapp also spoke with us, offering insight on IBM's Innov8 program. Steve Prentice, of Gartner Group, generously gave his time and valued opinion. We spoke with Persis Trilling of Princeton University in Second Life®, and Dr. Larry Johnson of the New Media Consortium, as well as Susan

Tenby, representing the Non-Profit Commons, and Simon Bignell of The University of Derby, UK. Several entrepreneurs are included in the book, each offering their personal stories and candid advice. We surrounded ourselves with virtual world topics by participating in events, attending conventions and meetings both in world and in real life. We met Sibley Verbeck of The Electric Sheep Company, and discussed the major brands they introduced to Second Life® and to other virtual worlds. We also had the good fortune to speak with Mitch Kapor, famed Lotus Notes creator and Linden Lab® investor. One of our most noteworthy meetings was with Second Life® creator Philip Rosedale. Thank you for answering every one of my e-mails, even when you were fresh off "the Playa." I am very grateful.

There are many people to thank for helping us on our virtual world journey and with the publication of this book. There were countless conversations, which prompted bigger questions and sparked great ideas, many of which were acted upon. Kathey and Michael Fatica have our love and appreciation. We are so fortunate to have you in our lives, real and virtual. There are hundreds to mention, but we were told to keep it to a minimum, so here it goes: Thank you Katydid Something, Gilly Gully, Chester Cournoyer, Mia Kitchensink, Chestnut Rau, Zha Ewry, Posableman Hold, Gunnar Bekkers, Clarissa Dassin, Mark Barrett, Scope Cleaver, Keystone Bouchard, Kiwini Oe, Persis Trilling, Poid Mahovlich, Liam Kanno, Bjorlyn Loon, Alliez Mysterio, Veronica Brown, Randall Moss, Sheet Spotter, Robert69 Little, Kayosan Tully, Sumtra Oh, John Fischer, Jeemy Winkler, Kenedi Winkler, Autohaus Winkler, Rogelio Klees, Lucki Eberhardt, Izzy Lemon, Kellie Kegan, Nancy Byrne, Jane Cusmano, Mike Martin, Elizabeth Martin, every member of Molaskey's Pub, Pub Crawlers of Second Life®, Metanomics, Torley Linden, Hamlet Au, Joe Linden, Pathfinder Linden, Phoenix Linden, Red Linden, Catherine Linden, Teeple Linden, Grace Buford a.k.a. Cylindrian Rutabaga, Filthy Fluno a.k.a. Jeffrey Lipsky, Lyndon Heart, TallGuy Kidd a.k.a. Dale Marsh, Capos Calderwood a.k.a. Alex Whitmore, Skinny Shepherd a.k.a. Alex Bevan, Harleen Gretzky, Greenfield Walcott, Bunny Costello, Glitteractica Cookie a.k.a. Susan Tenby, Cybergrrl Oh a.k.a. Aliza Sherman, Brian Regan, Harry Menta of the Small Business Administration, John Mahon, Sibley Verbeck, Giff Constable, Mark Guan at IBM®, and Steve Prentice, to name a few.

For Joëlle Delbourgo, our literary manager: Thank you for putting this into action. Thanks for clearing a path and for your timing and professionalism and guidance. To the editors at AMACOM, especially Jacqueline Flynn, Jennifer Holder, and Mike Sivilli. Thank you, Jacquie, for taking us on and trusting us. And to Jennifer and Michael for helping us reach the goal line.

We are fortunate enough to have many friends——you know who you are ;). It is impossible to list each one. We both have life-long friends, and new friends that feel like old friends. Your inspirational words, excitement, and positive energy really helped us keep the momentum going when we needed it. And there were times when we needed it.

To James and Sean, for being part of it all.

—Sue Martin Mahar
and Jay Mahar

PART 1.

ABOUT SECOND LIFE®

1.

Genesis of
Life Online

While the idea of a functioning virtual world has been with him since he started programming computers in the fourth grade, Philip Rosedale made the virtual world a reality when he introduced Second Life® to the public in 2003 through his company, Linden Lab®. Now, even with improved visual display, navigation, and increasing popularity, Second Life® is still in its developmental years. In many ways, it's just like watching the Internet evolve into Web 2.0.

The Internet was initially misunderstood as being a complex tool for the high-tech niche market. But as Internet companies formed and grew, they released user-friendly technology that opened worlds of communication possibilities and simplified things for the masses that would soon follow. Not until computers were widely used in offices, stores, libraries, schools, and the general marketplace did the Internet become a common part of our culture. The general public embraced the Net as an essential personal tool for information, for communication, for shopping, and especially for building and marketing businesses.

Just as the Internet prompted us to think outside the box, virtual worlds—and Second Life® in particular—will prompt innovation and creativity as you begin to think about your business in entirely new ways. A key way Second Life® changes how we use the Internet is that, through a 3D simulator, it provides the platform for real-time interaction in a virtual-world environment. What makes this so appealing for business? You can use Second Life® to:

- Market real-world products or services.

- Sell virtual-world products or services.

- Participate as a developer and owner, not just as a user.

The Search for Intelligent Life

Jay, my spouse and coauthor, joined Second Life® in June 2006 as avatar Apple MacKay when there were only about 235,000 members. I watched as he feverishly absorbed all he could about this 3D world. My first perception of Second Life® was that it was a bit desolate and raunchy, but I admit that my suspicious wife attitude was at work as I watched from over Jay's shoulder. He spent so much time in SL™, leaving me alone in the real world, that I decided I had to join him on this virtual-world journey. I had never played any computer games, never been in chat rooms, never had an interest in this kind of thing before. But Jay was spending a lot of time learning Second Life®, and his enthusiasm led to the proclamation that this was the future of the Internet. Hearing that, I decided there was nothing stopping me from getting a better understanding of it too. When I first logged on in August 2006, as Nasus Dumart, Second Life® had already grown to 403,000 members. With the careful guidance of Jay and his avatar Apple MacKay, I quickly realized why he was so excited: The potential was beyond anything I could have imagined.

Because creating this three-dimensional world takes an understanding of physics, mathematics, and social structuring, and because residents were responsible for building this amazing situation, there had to be intelligent life out there using it for something beyond gambling and sex. And I charged myself with finding it. I resolved that if I couldn't find people I liked, I was not wasting more time. I set out with high standards, and it didn't take long before they were met.

Using the Second Life® search tool, I used keywords, such as "university," "business," "museum," and city names like "Paris," "New York," "London," "Tokyo," and, yes, even "Hollywood." Using other keywords, I found dance halls, temples, cathedrals, art galleries, racetracks, classrooms, rain forests, and even the solar system. I also set out to find witty people to talk to. I am not sure how I found Three Lions Pub, built and owned by Phil Plasma, but I am sure glad I did. This was one of the first places I arrived at and felt immediately comfortable, without knowing another soul. The Pub was a breeding ground for situational comedy. The type-chat was as funny as any *Benny Hill Show*, *The Young Ones*, or any other BBC comedy hit.

Three Lions Pub was built when Phil Plasma was laid up at home recovering from a real-life accident. To alleviate his boredom, he joined Second Life® and built a place where he could enjoy a few laughs with friends. He established simple rules: introduce no commercialism of any kind, do not camp (leave your avatar unattended), respect others, and have fun. He built a traditional style English pub. Word caught on across the globe. English and European residents of Second Life® felt at home, along with a few U.S.-bred British junkies, just like me. People began volunteering their time to manage it at all hours, providing DJs, bouncers, hosts, and flocks of people. To Phil Plasma's surprise, Three Lions Pub in Burton Village, SL™ became one of the most popular social destinations in all of Second Life®.

Because this was definitely a U.K./Euro crowd, I found myself logging on to SL™ in my midday hours to catch some of the prime-time banter. That's when I realized that this is as interactive as entertainment gets. Giff Constable, Chief Operating Officer with The Electric Sheep Company, said, "If something shows it has an audience, it will be given a look. Entertainment companies in need of fresh ideas, take notice. The whole scene was wonderfully entertaining.

Hello Out There in Virtual Land

When I first heard Internet radio, with its live DJs and live performance, in Second Life®, I sensed it was an important and largely undiscovered medium.

In August 2006, when virtual life became a reality for me, there were fewer than half a million Second Life® residents, and barely 10,000 simultaneously logged on each day. Imagine being one of only thousands to experience broadcast television for the first time. I felt the same excitement and emotions the generations before me must have experienced seeing their first television program. Like the Internet, television was not popularized for decades after it was created. Though broadcast television was possible as early as 1928, radio programs remained the global entertainment standard through the Great Depression and World War II. By the 1950s, television reigned supreme. Most television programs during that time were broadcast live. In Second Life®, the term, "live" is also known as real-time. Not only can you hear a performance as you can with radio and see a live performance as in television, virtual worlds also allow you to interact, in real time, with the audience and with the performer. Using type-chat, I cheered for one such performer; then the performer, using a microphone, spoke directly to me. The first time I heard a performer say my avatar name, thanking me for a tip and attending the show, I nearly fell off my chair. Interaction makes all the difference.

After a few months of exploring, I began to tell close friends and family about this amazing and indescribable world called Second Life®. Word spread through the media too. Second Life® became a lively subject of conversation. No matter what a person's knowledge of virtual worlds was prior to speaking with me about my experiences, I detected a pattern of insatiable curiosity, discovery, and delight.

Second Life® has received so much press coverage that most people are not surprised when you talk about it anymore. In the May 14, 2007, edition of *Time Magazine*'s Most Influential People in the World—The Time 100, Philip Rosedale is featured under the category of Builders & Titans as a Master Builder of Second Life®'s Alternate Reality. *The New York Times* has been featuring articles about Linden Lab and Second Life® since 2004. The topics range from technology to job potential and relationships. Morning news programs like *The Today Show* and *CBS Sunday Morning* have demonstrated Second Life® for their audiences. It's even made its way into prime time television on CBS's popular program *CSI: NY* and NBC's hit, *The Office*. Second Life® has found its way into scripts, commercials, and books. Prior to these television cameos, demonstrations, and news articles, it used to be that you had to explain what an avatar was. Since the rise in popularity of Second Life® in 2007, that is hardly necessary anymore.

Internet 2.0

Second Life® is about to form a mass-market tidal wave. People with every background, interest, skill, and reason are creating a Second Life® avatar and exploring the Internet in 3D. Well-known establishments, such as IBM, are confidently leading the way into the Metaverse through Second Life®. To them, this is clearly the Internet 2.0. Other companies have begun or will soon require employees to maintain an avatar, just as they required employees to have an e-mail address in the 1990s.

Steve Prentice, lead analyst and Chief of Research with Gartner Group, the world's leading information technology research and advisory company, made a bold prediction: "By the end of 2011, as many as eighty percent of active Internet users will participate in and have as much interest in the 'virtual world' as they have with e-mail and Internet communication." When I queried him about this statement, he said, "that comment has received a lot of attention." And he firmly stands by it.

Virtual worlds are a collection of technologies serving many purposes. Their lifeline falls in tune with what Gartner Group calls The Hype Cycle. Using a chart calculating visibility and time, Gartner can gauge the life cycle of a new technology. This happens in five critical steps.

1. *Technology Trigger.* This is during product launch, or the breakthrough. A steep up curve on the chart indicates this stage.

2. *Peak of Inflated Expectations.* At this point, the technology is widely popular, at the height of the hype. This is indicated on the chart as the height of visibility.

3. *Trough of Disillusionment.* The product fails to meet the expectations generated by the hype and by its popularity. This is when the product loses its luster and the press abandons it as a hot topic. This phase is indicated on the chart with a down slope.

4. *Slope of Enlightenment.* The product regains its momentum, having learned from the previous stages of the Hype Cycle.

5. *Plateau of Productivity.* A steady flow of production carries it through time.

Steve explained that Second Life® had not yet reached the Plateau of Productivity, leaving it somewhere between the Trough of Disillusionment and Slope of Enlightenment. He does feel that Second Life® is heading to a long phase within the Plateau of Productivity, "once they mature and find their place."

If you are more familiar with other virtual-world technologies—such as the four major groups of virtual worlds: gaming, social networking, 'tween games, and intraverses (also known as private virtual worlds)—you might understand Second Life®'s placement better by comparing it.

1. *Online Gaming.* The gaming world, which includes a long list of variously themed games, has plateaued. Games have been on the market a long time and have consistently provided hundreds of millions of users with a predictable, entertaining platform.

2. *Social Networks.* Social networks, such as MySpace, FaceBook, Second Life®, and others, are beginning to peak in popularity. A long life-cycle is expected for them.

3. *'Tween Games.* The 'tween games are hugely popular. These include Neo Pets, Club Penguin, Habbo Hotel, and others. Generation I dominates this market with hundreds of millions of users. Steve Prentice claims this market is still on the upswing. Carefully moderated teen and preteen virtual worlds dwarf the adult virtual worlds in size and popularity.

4. *Intraverse.* The intraverse is a private platform virtual world used mainly for meetings and carefully guarded collaborative work environments separated from the community, or public virtual worlds. These are servers that are privately owned, created, and maintained by individuals or companies. They strictly require the owner's invitation to enter. The invitation may be offered as a temporary pass or for the long term. This sector has an interesting future, but it is still in development.

Steve Prentice feels that the future of virtual worlds includes interoperability, which occurs when systems of communication work together, creating a seamless crossover from one system to another. An example is a platform with the 3D immersive Second Life®, the networking ability of FaceBook, combined with the multimedia world of YouTube, creating a hybrid Web site and forum. Internet platforms, such as virtual worlds and multitiered communication systems, are expected to become interoperable.

According to Prentice, Generation I (those born during the onset of the Internet) will overwhelmingly prefer virtual worlds as a form of communication. Being raised with sophisticated technology, as this generation matures, they will embrace virtual worlds and the interoperability of all communication systems. Perhaps then, as they mature, we should consider them Generation I for *Interoperable*.

The Gartner Group is following Second Life®. Steve Prentice says it is equivalent to the "next big thing" in communication, as VisiCalc was in 1979. VisiCalc was the first spreadsheet program, which was adopted by Apple computer for business computing. It was a revolutionary tool, merging the technology industry with mainstream business. It led to refined programs, such as SuperCalc, Microsoft's MultiPlan, Lotus 1-2-3, Apple Works, and Excel. As the Second Life® platform is refined, it too will become widely accepted as a necessary global business tool.

According to several market analysts, people will be or are being introduced to Second Life® through their jobs, as happened with the Internet 20 years ago. An avatar is the modern-day equivalent to a standard company e-mail address, but with much more ability. For instance, your e-mail was never so mobile. Avatars can send and receive messages, but additionally they are a three-dimensional vehicle capable of interacting. Is your e-mail able to develop a personality, change its look, gesture, teleport from site to site, and take snapshots of places it has been? Your avatar can.

The wave is somewhat small now, but its size and strength have been building since 2003. As people become skilled in real-time 3D Internet navigation and user experience is improved, people will apply it in ways that work for them. This wave will continue to swell with each unique application.

Popularity certainly helps, but beyond the novelty, flexibility is what makes Second Life® the fastest growing virtual world. It is transforming the way we use the Internet.

Its Dé-jà vu All Over Again

Though Internet history is repeating itself, this time it will not take three decades for mainstream users to accept the "next big thing." That time lapse was largely due to the unavailability of equipment. In 1965, when the Internet was developed, the average person did not own a computer. Once the computer went from mainframe to mainstream, the Internet was utilized as a business and personal tool, creating opportunity and tremendous growth. But now, every mainstream computer user has sophisticated equipment, so creating a virtual-world presence is just a matter of downloading the Second Life® application and logging on.

Halfway through its first decade, Second Life® is carrying a dedicated population into a vast new existence that is known as the Metaverse. Through the recommendations and examples of respected leaders and innovators in various fields, more and more people are arriving to explore this 3D interactive space.

In October 2006, *Wired Magazine* posted an article correlating the development and growth of Second Life® with American history milestones. Second Life® pioneers faced a virgin frontier of digital space. These early settlers, especially the first million residents, built the foundations for Second Life®. They brought together their understanding of intellectual property, the virtual-world environment, and knowledge of social networks, and they took the chance to own virtual land (unheard of before Second Life®) and demonstrated their passion for making this world something special. Although many early residents were happy keeping Second Life® to themselves, it wasn't long before the increasing hype attracted millions of people who would want to join, bringing with them big business, or, in historical terms, carpetbaggers.

Just as the Declaration of Independence defines America, it could also define Second Life®. By stating that we are free to stand on our own—without monarchs, dictators, and self-empowered rulers of any kind—we are free to choose how to live our lives, real and virtual. This is a privilege and a right that not every person can claim in the real world. After meeting Philip Rosedale, I can confidently say that the world of Second Life® was created on a foundation of benevolence, giving power to the people through a love of physics, technology, and pure enthusiasm. And like America, Second Life® truly is built by the people, for the people.

Disruptive Innovation

Mitch Kapor, best known as the creator of 1982's Lotus 1-2-3 (which made the PC ubiquitous in business), is a well-known philanthropist and innovative technology leader who currently serves as founder, chair, or board member of several companies, including Linden Lab, Mozilla Foundation, Open Source Applications Foundation, Mitchell Kapor Foundation, Level Playing Field Institute, and Foxmarks. According to Mitch, the virtual-world Second Life® is a disruptive innovation. That is, it will "displace all (innovation) that had come before." The automobile, telephone, television, and steamship were all disruptive innovations in their time. Even mainframe computers of the 1970s were replaced by personal computers in the 1980s. A disruptive innovation is something so big and powerful that it changes, if not replaces, the previous innovation. He explains that with the Web and Internet going 3D, Second Life® is creating a kind of technology ecosystem that forces the reorganization of existing economic and social patterns. With Second Life®, "we are at the edge of the same phenomenon."

As Mitch points out, "standard businesses are not yet using virtual worlds. They are using video conferencing, travel, classrooms, etc. To replace that with 'virtual worlds' does not (yet) seem credible to Fortune 500 companies." But he goes on to add, "Those capabilities are going to grow and mature."

What Makes Second Life® Unique

A 3D real-time interactive online environment is nothing new. Since the 1990s, millions of people have accessed several online worlds. Most of those online worlds have been in the form of games, like Doom, Quake, Activeworlds, The Sims, and the like. Players log in and engage in battle or social interaction. What distinguishes Second Life® from other virtual worlds is that it allows its users to create a world—in 3D and in real time—while retaining ownership rights to their creations, and it also provides a viable monetary system. In other 3D online environments, which are created by a game developer, there is typically a goal to advance to higher levels and acquire the accessories needed for each new level, increasing virtual-world status. These fantasy virtual worlds fit in the category of hobby and entertainment with a distinguishable difference between virtual and real life. Second Life® is blurring the lines between the virtual world and the real world with its monetary system that converts into real-world currency, with its land and content ownership, and with its advances in depth perception cameras to mimic real-life movement. Philip Rosedale created the world of Second Life®, then invited the real world to participate.

With Second Life®, you can:

- Custom-build a virtual world.

- Retain rights to the things you create.

- Spend and earn real money.

Custom-Building a Virtual World

The software application known as the Second Life® viewer serves as your window onto the virtual world. It is what fills your computer screen with the immersive 3D quality. It equates to a 3D Web browser. This is a licensed, open source application, and the code to the Second Life® viewer is therefore accessible to everyone. That means you are able to customize your Second Life® viewer to suit the needs of a particular audience. The code has been released under GNU open source software license. By doing so you can modify the viewer and offer an entry point, or portal, to your landing spot, bypassing Linden Lab's Orientation Island. The responsibility is then upon you to orientate newcomers arriving at your location in Second Life®.

The Electric Sheep Company, a leading virtual-world production company, created a Second Life® viewer for their client, CBS. They had produced the virtual-world portion of CBS's popular prime time show *CSI:NY* in October 2007, drawing a large audience into Second Life®. The software application viewer, which they named OnRez, was designed with the *CSI:NY* audience in mind. It had virtual-world detective gadgets featured on the television program. It even offered avatars that looked like the television characters. When audience members logged on to Second Life® through the *CSI:NY*/Electric Sheep Company portal, they landed on the scene of the crime, role-playing to their sleuthing delight. Seasoned avatars were hired to assist these new arrivals. Although the *CSI:NY* project was temporary, it had lasting impact in the virtual world.

Several Second Life® communities welcome newcomers through their customized portal. It is a great way for people with like interests to find one another in this growing world. Several cities and countries, such as Brazil, Netherlands,

France, Italy, Dublin, Berlin, Tokyo, and Spain, have their own entrances into Second Life®. Anshe Chung is a well-known Second Life® developer who created Dreamland, specializing in business and entertainment-themed zones. Showtime's niche market television show, *The L Word*, has extended popularly into the virtual world. Nearly 30 communities have custom portals to choose from on the Second Life® Web site.

However, custom-creating a 3D viewer and entry point into Second Life® is not an option for everyone. It requires a high level of technical expertise. For everyone else, the standard issue Linden Lab viewer is perfectly sufficient for all your Second Life® needs.

Retaining Rights to the Things You Create

Second Life® is completely designed, built, improved upon, and owned by those who inhabit it. The rights to any literary, musical, and artistic creations [known as intellectual property rights (IPR)], belong to the creators. As long as you can prove you are the originator of a creative work, you have the right to license, sell, or give your work away. In the virtual world, your rights to your creations are protected as if they were physical property in the real world. Everything created in Second Life® retains the creator's avatar name, no matter how many times it is redistributed or sold. Copyrights, patents, trademarks, and trade secrets are included in IPR. Intellectual property rights make all the difference in the virtual-world (and real-world) economy. You own what you create.

Creators control how people can use their work by setting a permission type. Ownership of objects can be transferred, just as real-life artists sell their artwork or a furniture maker sells a sofa. Once a transaction is complete, whatever the terms, ownership can be transferred, but not creation origination. Permissions allow owners to trade, give away, or sell their attained objects. For example:

- You can allow people to freely copy a t-shirt with your company logo on it that they can then pass on to others. That's a giveaway, or a freebie.

- You can set permission for a temporary, special trade. For instance, Apple MacKay created a DJ booth that was admired by a game maker. Apple traded a DJ booth for a game table. Prior to giving one object to the other, both Apple MacKay and the game maker set permissions so that it could not be copied or sold. It was an even trade.

- You can duplicate your creations as many times as you want, with the proper setting of permissions. This is useful in vending systems. You don't have to replenish supplies; you can set it to generate automatically.

You don't have to worry about your creations being copied or stolen as long as you properly set permissions either to freely distribute them, like promotional pieces, or to sell them as unique and valuable commodities.

People who are skilled in 3-D building can create everything they need and are nearly, or virtually, self-sustaining. If you have the skill to create everything you will need and even sell what you make, you do not need to rely on another source to exist. Well, maybe that's a bit of a stretch. We all need something from someone, whether it's a skill or an object or companionship. Apple MacKay is a good example of a virtually self-sustaining skilled builder in Second Life®. He set a goal upon entering this 3D world. He wanted to build or create everything he needed. If he needed a building, he built it. If he wanted sunglasses, he made them. He started out with no money, like most start-ups, so essentially, in the beginning, he had no choice but to make all that he needed and wanted. Soon his 3D ability was noticed. He was commissioned to create for others. That earned him a Linden income. Without drawing any real-world dollars to establish himself in Second Life®, Apple MacKay has been sustaining a comfortable Second Life® by relying on his 3D skills, among other things.

In Second Life®, it is possible to own the rights to land. Virtual land ownership is not necessary for recreational use of Second Life®, but to obtain overall control of your business development, it is recommended. Do you rent your Web site or own it? Think of your Second Life® site as an Internet domain.

Second Life® is free to all, but to own land you must be a paying premium member (check the secondlife.com site for current rates). Renting is an option. You don't have to be a premium member or pay Linden Lab to rent property, but you are restricted to the owner's rules and the number of objects known as primitives, or prims, you are allowed to use on your rental property. (Prims are the number of parts a 3D object consists of.) Each computer simulator, or sim, can support only a certain number of prims to function properly.

Land parcels come as small as 512 square meters, which is 1/128 of a region. The maximum number primitives on a 512-square-meter parcel is 117. An entire region on the mainland is 65,536 square meters and supports 15,000 prims. Another option—one that is right for large projects and community building—is a private region, or island. Private islands are the same size and have the same prim allowance as an entire mainland region, but they offer privacy and greater simulator performance. This is because an entire simulator, or central processing unit (CPU) is dedicated to each island. You also have the option to add on to your region as your needs grow. Educational and nonprofit organizations are given a discount for purchasing an island.

Your virtual-world land is the equivalent of an Internet Web site, only with an immersive, 3D interactive ability. You wouldn't establish a business without a Web site these days, would you? Establishing a virtual-world presence for your business may soon become as common a practice as building a sophisticated Web site. As Web sites and domains have fluctuating market value, so does Second Life® real estate. Website addresses are found using a uniform resource locator (URL), In Second Life® you have a Second Life® URL, or SLurl™, which can be loaded onto a traditional Web site, linking visitors to your Second Life® location. Think of your Second Life® location as a 3D website that is also an intangible ownership.

As virtual land values increase and businesses are established, rights holders will even need to consider what to do with this asset in the event of a real-life death. It is possible to bequeath your account and your Second Life® to another resident in the event of death.

Spending and Earning Real Money

In Second Life®, property owners and residents have developed a system of commerce, created by a currency trade and a healthy sense of supply and demand. The Second Life® currency, known as Lindens, electronically converts to real-world money when you process it through the Linden™ exchange, PayPal, or other Internet monetary exchange systems. The Linden exchange, also known as the LindeX™, is a Linden Lab regulated monetary exchange system where Lindens can be exchanged for U.S. dollars at the going market rate maintained at about 270 Linden per 1 USD.

Linden Lab offers current economic reports on their Web site, *http://secondlife .com/whatis/economy_stats.php*. They provide information, helping virtual-world inquisitors understand the economic status of Second Life®. They offer up-to-date information on Second Life® population, land sales, Linden dollar activity, monthly user hours, and other useful statistics. When you're building a business, it is important to have this kind of information handy. In July 2008, it was stated that the Second Life® in-world economy is continuing to grow, generating $330 million annually. No other virtual world can claim that rate of growth. Second Life® is unique not only in the economic and creative power it gives people, but in how people are using it.

Top Five Practical Uses for Second Life®

Although you have the ability to fly, have the body of a god or goddess, look cool, and meet other people in Second Life®, that's not what no-nonsense business folk are after in Second Life®. It comes down to practical use. Companies and universities that are building in Second Life® wouldn't spend their time there if it didn't prove to be a valuable tool on many levels. The benefits of participating in Second Life® are:

- Interacting in the third and fourth dimensions
- Providing an economical and ecological substitute to business travel

- Enjoyment

- The ability to multitask

- Serving as a collaborative work platform

Interacting in the Third and Fourth Dimensions

The third dimension is depth of field. Depth is created in a simulator, where you can maneuver your view around 360 degrees. In the third dimension, you are represented in a digital form—an avatar—with the ability to digitally interact with the people and objects around you.

The fourth dimension, which is often overlooked, represents social connections. According to Grady Booch (IBM Fellow and Chief Scientist, Rational Software, IBM Corp.), "When we connect with others, we are exchanging intellectual and social compatibility. The fourth dimension introduces the human factor."

The fourth dimension involves the most distinguishing feature of virtual-world avatars and their interaction within the world: human personality. Personality comes through easily interacting with your custom-made avatar. You create a look, but you also exude your intelligence and personal style through spoken language, chat, and gestures.

An Economical and Ecological Substitute to Business Travel

At a time when we are reconsidering how we live and conduct business, making ecosensible and budget-conscious choices in every move we make, the real world will consider the virtual world a practical and sensible alternative for business meetings. When you opt for the virtual-world meeting instead of a traditional business trip, you're accomplishing effective interaction with your colleagues and clients without incurring any costs of travel, rearranging your schedule (or the schedule of your family), exhausting your energy, or creating consumer waste associated with being on the go.

Enjoyment

When people admit that one advantage to Second Life® is that it is fun and interesting, I feel like I'm hearing a confession. Nevertheless, third on the list is the fun factor. Fun, interesting, and novel experiences are an important part of business user activity.

You're able to keep linked to the lighter side of life when having a real conversation with someone wearing a space suit. It also takes the edge off when you meet with someone who stands up at a meeting, only to turn around and walk into a wall. A mistake like that somehow makes a person appear human. That's just a virtual-world technicality, not an embarrassing social faux pas. That kind of situation is perfectly normal in Second Life®, and it can be funny. Without doubt, humor has a place in Second Life®. You can do things in the virtual world that are impossible in the real world. Having superhuman abilities can be a lot of fun.

There's plenty to do and see in Second Life®. You can expand relationships through Second Life® outings. There are quality art museums, live music concerts, and parties to attend. People can explore the cultural side of virtual life while building business bridges. Sometimes the best business connections come from social situations.

Second Life® is, after all, a social network.

The Ability to Multitask

The fourth and most practical use of Second Life® is the ability to multitask. Conducting meetings, conferences, and training seminars in a virtual environment often result in enhanced efficiency because people don't need to leave their desks.

Knowledge Is Power

When the Internet was ready for commercial use, businesses scrambled to train their employees to use essential office tools such as PowerPoint, Excel, Word, and e-mail. E-mail, of course, became a standard in modern-day communication. Web site addresses and e-mail addresses began to appear on business cards and office stationery around the world. Once people got the hang of using search engines to navigate the Web, the computer became even more personal, user-friendly, and professional. Your online business skills were likely acquired from professional training and practice.

As they evolve and however you refer to them—Internet 2.0, 3D Internet—virtual worlds like Second Life® may become as widely used as television, the World Wide Web, or any medium we know and use everyday.

One of the biggest and most influential business developers in Second Life® is IBM (http://IBM.com). With its history in developing the original World Wide Web for commercial use through code, software, hardware, services, and business development and with a thorough understanding of the workings of the Internet, IBM is a real-life global business leader paving the way to virtual worlds. IBM has been using virtual worlds as a daily business tool long before the general population thought of it as anything more than a game. The virtual world has become a means of communication so vital that a great majority of IBM employees have avatars with which to log on and instantly connect with one another despite geographic differences.

Though it may be back to the drawing board to learn a new online program, you won't regret having the knowledge and skills. Taking the time now to learn about real-time 3D virtual worlds may save you from playing catch-up later.

Impact of Virtual Worlds

Global communication has gone from the telegraph to the telephone to the Internet to 3D interactive virtual worlds. Each innovation improved on its communication predecessor, spawning new businesses with the allure of speed, ease, and functionality. Second Life® is the next level of global communication. As real-time 3D technology improves and as users become more virtual savvy, Second Life® (and similar emerging virtual worlds that are likely to follow in its footsteps) will be used for daily business and communication, and it will be regarded as a money-saving and money-making tool. With these uses, 3-D Internet virtual worlds have the ability to significantly transform industry. Communication in the virtual world will impact everyone, not just a specific group of Internet entrepreneurs.

2.

A Virtual Melting Pot

Second Life® means different things to different people. For some, the name suggests a detached cyber existence in which people leave the real world behind, trading their everyday interactions for virtual ones. Though that may be true for some role-playing residents, it is not the same experience for everyone. For a large majority, role-playing has nothing to do with their reasons for using Second Life®. These people enjoy the global interaction, with people who represent almost every demographic, culture, degree of education, fetish, profession, and personality. Despite their diversity, the people of Second Life® have successfully achieved a self-governing, highly functioning global community respectful of everyone's differences. There is no war in Second Life®, nor are there disease or racial, gender, or age discrimination. This 3D interactive virtual world is what you make of it, and the residents have chosen an open, inclusive lifestyle. As the Second Life® slogans say, "Your World, Your Imagination" and "Your World, Your Way." In this way, it is a twenty-first century virtual melting pot on a global scale.

Live a Second Life® on Second Life®

One of the earliest attractions people had to Second Life® was the ability to live an alternate lifestyle. Along with developing amazing virtual world structures, you can also develop an online persona through your avatar, who is known only in the virtual world. Privacy in Second Life® is self-protected. No one needs to know your real life if you don't want it known. The mystery of the person behind the avatar is part of the intrigue. You could be an international superstar in the real world, recognized instantaneously wherever you go, but in the virtual world of Second Life®, you can choose to be an average person. In contrast, you could be an average person in the real world and a superstar in the virtual world.

I have met several people in Second Life® who have some real-life notoriety. They choose to keep their real life and custom-made virtual life separate. Being a music promoter at Molaskey's Pub in Second Life®, I know musicians who have headlined or toured with real-life big-name bands. They don't use their real-life fame in the virtual world. For them, it is an opportunity to do what they love: perform live music, without the expectations of being a celebrity overshadowing them.

Celebrities are not the only ones hiding in plain sight. Executives who have built their real life on corporate protocol are using Second Life® as an outlet to fulfill hobbies in music, art and design, and other interests. I have learned that a talented musician in Second Life® is a real-life, high-powered media executive. I will always first think of her as a talented musician, because that is how I was introduced to her. I also met someone in Second Life® who lost their real-life job as a legislative coordinator. She reinvented herself in Second Life® taking a whole new career path as a real estate developer. Another person is redefining himself as a talented machinimatographer, the virtual world equivalent of a real-life videographer. Everyone has a story. The virtual world is where people can be themselves, reinvent themselves, or define themselves, letting the world sample them for who they are—based on the content of their character.

A conversation on anonymity in Second Life® often rises. A Second Life® friend once said, "You never know whom you are talking with in Second Life®." The real-life person behind the avatar you are making small talk with could be Maya Angelou, Steve Jobs, an heiress, or even someone from around your hometown. I suspect my friend is someone with her own real-life notoriety, which she guards.

On another note, avatars may try to impress you with their material goods. Mansions and jewelry are relatively simple to acquire in Second Life®. Don't be so easily impressed. You can live out quite a lifestyle in the virtual world while your real life may afford you only meager accommodations. That's one of the attractions of the virtual world. You can retreat to your mansion in the sky right from the comfort of your cramped city apartment, for example.

For those looking for notoriety, the virtual world offers the opportunity to tell everyone who you are, expanding your online presence. Whenever a big-name company comes to Second Life®, it makes the news. And with so much interest in the developing virtual world, people are interested in who is in the virtual world and how they are using it.

Notable Second Life® Communities

The groups in Second Life® define the communities. As an individual avatar or as a business, you can form and maintain a group or join an established one. While the categories of business groups are not formally defined, they can be generalized as:

- nonprofit.
- design and architecture.
- entertainment.
- arts.
- education.

(Second Life® is off-limits for minors, but it does offer a carefully monitored Second Life® Teen Grid for those between 13 and 18.)

Nonprofit

One of the strongest communities in Second Life® consists of the nonprofit organizations. To support them in their virtual efforts, Linden Lab offers a 50% discount on land purchases to verified real-world 501(c)3 nonprofit organizations, educators, and academic institutions that will be using the regions to support their organization's official work.

The majority of nonprofits are united in a group called The Non-Profit Commons, founded by Susan Tenby, a senior manager for online community development with Tech Soup (techsoup.org). Tech Soup is a nonprofit organization that provides technology solutions to other nonprofit organizations. In December 2004, Susan Tenby established The Non-Profit Commons, the first nonprofit establishment in Second Life®.

When Linden Lab invited Susan to speak at a virtual world conference in 2005, she described her vision to create a place in Second Life® where nonprofit organizations can go for help in applying Second Life® to their needs. After hearing her speak at the conference, virtual real estate investor, Ailin Graef, also known as Anshe Chung, the first virtual-world real estate millionaire, approached Susan and praised her for her work. Ailin Graef then donated an entire island in Second Life® to Susan Tenby in support of her efforts with nonprofit organizations. The donated island is known as The Nonprofit Commons.

In The Non-Profit Commons (NPC), nonprofit, 501(c) organizations can establish a free Second Life® presence, receive virtual-world guidance, connect, attend events, sponsor events, and reach a global audience by way of networking, podcasting, participating in press events, and more. The NPC group is exclusively for residents, supporters, and volunteers of the NPC sim.

The Non-Profit Commons holds weekly meetings, monitored by Susan Tenby's avatar, Glitteractica Cookie. They are attended by dozens of avatars representing well-known and start-up organizations. They discuss how to use Second Life® to their fullest potential, often inspiring uncertain newcomers to shed their fears of "life in the virtual lane." In this nonprofit community, residents openly ask questions, network, and collaborate on projects. They accomplish more than any of them could have imagined when they signed onto Second Life®, except, of course, for Susan.

Susan realized Second Life®'s potential for networking early on. Through hard work, dedication, and a solid understanding of using technology for the advancement of nonprofit organizations, Susan has been able to establish a strong presence for all nonprofits in Second Life®.

Susan supplements the nonprofit groups in Second Life® with her Google Groups. When not in-world, everyone remains in contact through e-mail chat, which is very effective. Announcements are made, and invitations are sent for lectures, presentations, public relations, help requests, and more. It is one of the best networking systems established anywhere for any group. By using technology to communicate, nonprofit organizations—many on low budgets—are able to take great strides toward accomplishing their goals.

Many are surprised to learn that nonprofit organizations, philanthropists, and fund-raisers are using Second Life® as well as they are. In fact, using Second Life® makes perfect sense for nonprofit organizations, philanthropists, and fund-raisers, who thrive within strong communities. So Tech Soup's success in Second Life® is no surprise.

One of the single most popular nonprofit organizations in Second Life® is the American Cancer Society. Randall Moss, known in Second Life® as RC Mars, is a tech strategist with the American Cancer Society (ACS). He spoke with me about how the ACS is successfully using Second Life®. Randy is determined to create a consistent experience between the virtual world and the real world. The ACS often has mixed-reality fund-raising because it works so well.

The Relay for Life event in Second Life® is organized by Randall Moss, along with Jade Lilly. Jade contributed the skills to create American Cancer Society kiosks that were placed in dozens of places around Second Life®. As Randy Moss notes, the kiosks needed to be specially designed so that donations go directly to a master account at the American Cancer Society. Jade did a fantastic job of accomplishing that, stating "It was a tricky process of back-end-coding, but they successfully deposit every donated $L from Second Life®, which converts to US dollars, directly to the American Cancer Society."

In 2004, Jade Lily independently raised $2,000 for the American Cancer Society during a silent auction. With that kind of potential evident, they held the first Relay for Life event the following year and every year since. In 2005, they raised $5,000. In 2006, they raised $41,000. In 2007, they passed their goal and raised $168,500.

In the Relay for Life, the American Cancer Society has one of the most successful annual fund-raising events in Second Life®. The Relay for Life is a walk-a-thon that raises millions of dollars each year from thousands of participants. It is an 18- to 24-hour virtual-world avatar walk-a-thon. It begins in the spring with the disbursement of kiosks and material to participating venues. The season concludes in the summer, when avatars hit the virtual streets.

Design and Architecture

The structures and landscape in Second Life® are built by the many talented and skilled 3D builders. Some of them are real-life designers and architects, using Second Life® for its 3D modeling functions. The designers and builders in Second Life® have joined together, forming a community that relies on each other for critique, challenges, friendship, and professional advancement.

When I met with Keystone Bouchard (http://www.studiowikitecture.com, http://www.archsl.wordpress.com), at the advice of Persis Trilling, he had just completed a collaborative architecture project to design a telemedical center for a poor village in Nepal. The completed designs were part of the Open Architecture Challenge. Forty people had worked together in Second Life® to create a single design concept, using the 3D wiki technology they had developed. They submitted a design to be used by Nyaya Health. The results were on display at Arcspace Island, next to Architecture Islands, both owned by Keystone Bouchard.

Keystone Bouchard, whose real name is Jon Brouchoud, demonstrated Wikitecture and the Wiki Tree, explaining where architecture collaborators submit their design ideas. The Wiki Tree, which is a conceptual tree, has leaf spheres, each of which contains a different architectural design submitted for review. You simply click on a leaf sphere to view a design. Within seconds, the fully constructed selected design automatically appears on the lawn before you, ready for you to walk into and around it. Allowing enough time to walk about and discuss it, the building returns itself to the Wiki Tree in the form of a leaf sphere.

Real-life designs created in Second Life® are critiqued by architectural peers, improved, and remodeled. The Wiki Tree accepts critiques, color-coding the leaf spheres according to best and worst. Members of the community may also vote on what they like or dislike. The leaf colors are derived based on their popularity. Bright green ones are very popular, dark red ones not so popular. The tree then prunes itself of the worst designs, leaving only the best as options for further development. As many as 40 people have cooperated on a single project. They were able to create something far greater than anyone could have done alone.

As Jon Brouchoud has stated, "The community is continuing to improve the scripts and do things I could never have imagined." He continued, "Virtual architecture may also be the ultimate in green design. The more virtual environments become lifelike, and the higher the embedded energy cost of presence gets, the more virtual environments might become a means toward sustainability." Keystone Bouchard, Jon's avatar, came to Second Life® in June 2006. He saw Second Life® as a tool to help clients visualize design ideas for green residential projects from his real-life studio, Crescendo Design.

Operating from a studio located in the middle of nowhere, they were servicing clients from a broad geographic region. Using Second Life® made perfect sense. They could model design concepts from their office, and clients could check out the designs from the comfort of their homes, for as long as they want.

Taking that a step farther, their clients are able to test paint colors, material types and finishes, and even furniture layouts and landscaping options. If they want, they can do the entire project in Second Life®. For example, a client was living in London, planning to build a home in Wisconsin, but wouldn't be moving back for several months. The people at Crescendo Design told him about Second Life® and met him in-world. They built a replica of his land and started designing in SL. They had already gone through several design iterations on his virtual world site before ever meeting him in real life.

Jon's early work in Second Life® was done from building in public sandboxes until, Jon explained, "A naked avatar started harassing my client. That's the day I placed the order for my first island. I own two islands now. Both are incubators where I rent land to newbie architects and designers who want to explore the use of SL™ as a part of their research or professional applications."

Jon independently built a community for all the newbie architects coming and going through Second Life®. He rents them land for exactly what he pays for it. It doesn't cost him anything except time. He also holds several presentation events for architects: Cameron Sinclair from Architecture for Humanity, Sergio Palleroni from Basic Initiative, Chris Luebkeman from ARUP, Phil Bernstein from Autodesk, and other participators. It's a place where architects get to know other architects. As Jon pointed out, "SL is all about the community. It's a kind of social experiment I suppose."

With ambitious plans when he first started, Jon has become attached to doing purely virtual architecture, and he has nearly completely transitioned to virtual practice. In his Crescendo Design Studio in Second Life®, you can purchase one of several stylish designs and blueprints for a real-world Green Home, which are available for L$150,000 each (about $500).

What is a Green Home? Jon explains that each home is truly unique. "One example would be a client whose primary focus is energy. They may not be as concerned with sustainability, but want low utility bills. We see this as a shade of green, equally as important, and needing to be served as effectively as a client who wishes to engage in an extensive range of environmentally friendly principles."

Jon uses Second Life® to design high-quality, innovative, efficient structures and collaborates with other architects to create the best designs for both the virtual world and the real world. He says, "It's a really curious thing from an architectural perspective." He spends about 20 hours per week actually building. At age 32, making a comfortable living from his Second Life® business, Jon says, "It pays better than real-life architecture."

The way Jon Brouchoud looks at it, Second Life® is like working with a cardboard or clay study model. You can't expect exact precision, but you can depict the relationships between spaces and the overall aesthetic of a space, even if it isn't precise.

Jon Brouchoud and his peers were approached by the U.S. House of Representatives to build Capitol Hill in Second Life® for Congressman George Miller's presentation. It's also where Newt Gingrich gave a presentation, but it was originally built for the swearing in of the United States House of Representative, Nancy Pelosi. They also had some publicity for the Gallery of Reflexive Architecture. All the scripts used to make those installations were open sourced, so it just keeps spreading and getting bigger.

When the SL environment matures, is more stable, is less laggy with improved graphics, the Architecture group will go from 600 members to 60,000—a big jump in participation.

One of the architects and designers with an impressive portfolio in Second Life® is Scope Cleaver (www.Scopecleaver.com). SL™-Scope prefers to keep his real life completely separate from Second Life®, and for him it is entirely possible. "Scope should get all the attention," he said.

I spoke with Scope Cleaver after experiencing the concert hall at SL™-Princeton University, which he designed and built in about two months. Because it was an abstract structure, I asked him to settle a debate I was having with Apple MacKay. I said the structure looked like a goose, Apple said it looked like it had gills and being over the water, it must be a fish. Scope was amused with our debate. He said it has even been called garlic. We laughed at the possibilities. That's what Scope's designs and structures in Second Life® are about: possibilities.

A group of people making up a movement in SL say, "SL shouldn't be inspired by real life." Scope Cleaver subscribes to that notion because he understands that the idea is to go beyond real-life abilities, saying, "The idea is to promote new ways of thinking."

"What's interesting to witness," Scope continues, "is that the same group of people are those who want to identify something that looks abstract as a real thing—i.e., garlic, a big shrimp, etc. So they end up trying to make sense of it no matter what."

Scope Cleaver works in Second Life® full time, creating some of the most amazing architectural and design content there. I have no idea what he does in real life. He could be a descendant of Frank Lloyd Wright or a simple mason with great building sensibilities. His Second Life®, however, reveals that he has a firm grasp on creating virtual world content. He is booked one year in advance. Since he closely guards his real life, he wouldn't disclose what kind of money he is earning from his Second Life® business, but my guess is that he is living a comfortable real-life based on his Second Life® skills.

Jon Brouchoud remarked, "I think there's an opportunity to develop a new language of virtual architecture, free from the constraints of physical architecture—based purely on the inherent or native characteristics of this environment—that's really where the future lies for architects in virtual environments."

Entertainment

Prime-time television viewers are trading their television viewing time for interactive entertainment in a custom-made world. Actors, musicians, comedians, gamers, and partygoers make up a large population of Second Life® residents. There are so many groups and concurrent Second Life® events that drawing a crowd to an organized function requires talent.

Though live music seems to make up a large majority of the entertainment community, you can also find entertainment in the form of Shakespearian theater, stand-up comedy, virtual theme parks, parties, and plenty of role-playing, such as pirates, vampires, historic figures, and the like. The entertainment communities are dependent on keeping their audience interested, therefore drawing traffic to sites.

The live music scene in Second Life® is one of the most vibrant forms of entertainment. When the workday is done, almost everyone agrees that there's fun to be found in Second Life®. Listed in the top five most practical uses for Second Life® was "just for the fun of it."

The interactive chat between performer and audience makes everyone laugh out loud and gives a reason to gather again and again. Musicians often work an avatar's name into their song to the audience's delight. As I have stated before, the live music scene in Second Life® is an interactive experience like no other. These cyber concerts have been gaining a loyal and diverse following. With each of the talented performers, you see, hear, and sense the excitement. In this global community, there's likely a performance of some kind happening somewhere in every time zone. When you attend a live music event at Molaskey's Pub or anywhere else in Second Life®, you bring the show to yourself. It's is a great way to adopt a global lifestyle.

The music world in Second Life® is serious business. For all the events and gatherings happening—with 50,000 logged in at any one time—there is likely a live concert being performed somewhere, generating several thousand L$ an hour for the musician. Musicians with a following are paid L$5,000 plus tips for a one-hour show. When you calculate the exchange rate on that (assuming L$270 per $1USD), a musician with a Second Life® following is earning about L$25,000 a week for an average of four or five one-hour shows. That adds up to about L$100,000 a month, which is about $375USD a month for playing 16 to 20 hours of music—over $20 an hour. That's not bad for part-time work on your computer. For the musicians, they're relaxed enough in Second Life® that they consider playing in the virtual world a rehearsal for their real-life gigs. They're happy to do it, and they get paid to boot. For venue owners, it's a bargain for driving traffic to your site.

The Arts

Hundreds of artists have formed groups in Second Life®. Very often, they collaborate on projects, share information, or simply get to know one another. SL art is an emerging market. With the amount of creativity available through Second Life®, it is not surprising to learn that artists are creating original sculptures, exhibits, and photographs created entirely in Second Life®. These works are often put on display in public areas, private locations, virtual shops, and virtual museums. Although they can be seen on Web sites, television, and the like, visiting these original works in their natural 3-D state is a new experience. The modern art world has evolved.

Museum artifacts cannot be replicated in the virtual world unless they maintain an intellectual quality. There has been discussion about replicating masterpieces for the virtual world, but the conclusion so far is that representation is not art.

Museums

There are several museums in Second Life®, including:

- Virtual Starry Night—Vincent's Second Life® (http://www.skribeproductions .com/blog/2008/04/28/checking-out-virtual-starry-night/)

- International Space and Flight Museum (http://slispaceflightmuseum.org/ blog/)

- Star Trek Museum of Science (http://www.sabrizain.org/startrek/)

- Noah's Ark and Museum

- Abyss Museum of Ocean Science (http://abyss-secondlife.blogspot.com/)

- Tech Museum of Innovation (http://www.thetech.org/)

- Museum of Music (MuseumofMusic.org)

- NASA JPL on Explorer Island (http://www.nasa.gov/centers/ames/ multimedia/images/2008/future_forums_ 200 8.html)

- Globe Theatre (http://globe.sliterary.com/)

- SL Historical Museum

- and many more

The Exploratorium, in San Francisco, is a museum of science, art, and human perception, www.exploratorium.edu. This popular interactive museum has found a comfortable home in Second Life®, attracting visitors from around the world to experience virtual-world sensory perception, geosciences, video presentations, and lectures.

Education

Second Life® has a lot to offer academic circles. The very basis of SL incorporates the disciplines of science, social sciences, arts, physics, geology, political science, and technology, to name a few. One of the best examples of optimum usage is Princeton University.

New Media Consortium

The New Media Consortium (NMC) Virtual World in Second Life® (http://sl.nmc.org) is responsible for developing the strongest intellectual virtual community not only in Second Life®, but in the Metaverse. Doctor Larry Johnson, CEO of NMC, is known in-world as Larry Pixel. Larry spoke with me about how they use Second Life®.

The New Media Consortium was founded in 1993 by a group of publishers, hardware manufacturers, and software developers that became multimedia visionaries. The group sought to inspire and enable innovators from select universities to interact, collaborate, and effectively demonstrate successful applications of emerging technologies. Today, the NMC is a group of over 250 leading universities, museums, and learning initiative corporations collaboratively seeking and using new technologies.

With approximately 10,000 combined Web and virtual world members, the NMC is the largest educational network of its kind. They meet at conferences, interact, and communicate regularly. They typically find an interesting project and make an initiative to explore it, researching and identifying emerging technologies. That's how they found Second Life®.

The New Media Consortium is in other virtual worlds, but there is a big difference between a prebuilt virtual world and a user-built virtual world. The difference between, say, There.com and Second Life® has mainly to do with the tools. You can interact with others in any virtual world, but a prebuilt virtual world is not applicable to learning. Second Life® offers in-world tools for creating and communicating. This feature makes for a better learning environment.

The creative, communication, and collaborative abilities are among the key reasons Second Life® has become a fast growing success. For an organization like the New Media Consortium, having a resourceful virtual world in which to network, brand, present, collaborate, and create is pivotal in carrying out their mission.

The NMC holds several conferences a year, with a variety of topics and presenters. The virtual-world conferences were every bit as successful as real-life conferences because they are cost-effective. According to Dr. Johnson, all NMC events and conferences are now held entirely in Second Life®.

From the beginning, the NMC's basic business model has been to construct high-end sims where they could expand the learning experience and provide resources for their members and guests. Visitors can explore and utilize the NMC campus in Second Life® as they like. Members hold events in public spaces. Scheduling public space is successfully managed on their Web site by Google calendar. At the time of my interview with Dr. Johnson, NMC has 100 islands, half of which are client owned. These islands are privatized for elite NMC clients and NMC conferences. Only a few are public areas.

SL™-NMC is largely sustained by their popular networking conferences and high-end development services. In keeping with their nonprofit requirements, they also give back to the community by donating land for developing education, art, and culture in Second Life®. The NMC has made 30 4,096-square-meter parcels of land available for advanced learning exploration and use by selected members.

Although the NMC offers high-end development of simulators and virtual world consulting, they are at the low end of the pricing scale. They offer professionally developed islands to universities, museums, and learning initiative companies for about half of what large corporate developers charge.

The talented, intellectual virtual world developers at NMC are the best at replicating real-world buildings, such as the one with their well-known client, Princeton University. They are also the company to which world-class museums turn for discussing the development of virtual world museums, such as the SL™-MOMA.

Princeton University

Princeton University is one of eight universities in the Ivy League. Founded in 1746, the school recognizes Second Life® for its creativity, collaborative work abilities, and strong community. In 2007, SL™-Persis Trilling and her team at Princeton University Education Technologies Center opened a beautifully executed replica of the real-life Princeton University campus (http://etc.princeton.edu/sl/).

The spectacular buildings and campus, which took about four months of part-time work, was built with a team of Second Life® builders and designers, including CJ Carnot of the New Media Consortium Virtual Worlds team, and Scope Cleaver, whom Persis Trilling states is arguably the best builder in SL. There are eight islands: North, East, South, West, Forrestal, Groups, Alexander Beach, and Princeton University proper. Four of the eight are planned for later use.

The SL™ -Princeton University welcome area has replicated several buildings from the historic Princeton campus. The buildings chosen represent turning points in Princeton University history.

- The first structure is Nassau Hall, when the College of New Jersey was invited by Princeton to build there in 1756.

- The central building is Chancellor Green Library, the first freestanding library on campus and a very modern building at the time in 1873 (also using the first gaslight in the town).

- Alexander Hall was built when the College of New Jersey changed its name to Princeton University in 1896.

The design and campus layout are not a literal representation of the real-world campus, just fairly good ones, Persis proudly explained as we toured the campus. "They have succeeded in establishing the institutional brand and the spirit of the university in Second Life® without its being an exact replica."

One of the exploration goals Princeton established when planning their presence in Second Life® was to use it for classes, research, and community outreach. Although there is no distance education at all at Princeton University, the Second Life® experience augments the face-to-face classroom experience.

SL™-Princeton University sponsors many art and music events. Persis recognizes that "There are some amazing artists in Second Life®," and Alexander Hall is an amazing concert hall. It is an acoustically perfect structure and visually stunning.

A new center is opening at Princeton University that will create art that is said to be born digital, and it will exhibit original digital artwork and astonishing immersive art installations. DynaFleur is one such exhibit, located in the Princeton South region. Douglas Story and Desdemona Enfield created beautiful larger-than-life abstract floral photography. This is complemented by a special landscape created by SL™-Poid Mahovlich and by sound movement designed by SL™-Dizzy Banjo, remarkably created to respond to your presence as you walk through it.

PARSEC is another innovative, immersive virtual world art installation on display at SL™-Princeton. PARSEC is an interactive instrument using seven avatars that control music and objects using only their voice. There is even a challenge to unlock a puzzle within the musical composition, using level voice tones and a display of intellect. This is another one of Dizzy Banjo's compositions with Eshi Otawara as the creator of the PARSEC environment. The scripts are from Chase Marellan, a well-known programmer and author of many programming books, including the *Platform Second Life: Developing Real Life Applications* (Manning Press) with Jay Clarke.

The art at Princeton University is for display only. In fact, they don't sell anything at SL™-Princeton. Even the store stocks free items. You can visit the SL™-Princeton store in their Forrestal region and pick up a fairly decent-looking ready-made avatar, Princeton banners, clothing, accessories, and a New User Learning Tour HUD absolutely free.

One of the best kept secrets about Princeton University is the opportunity to hear 15 years worth of public lectures. They're free through University Channel for downloading to your iTunes, Podcasts, and Vodcasts. They will also be available through SL™-Princeton University.

The Princeton Groups region is the gathering spot for alumni, campus community, guests, research participants, student groups, organizations, environmental awareness, and the build group.

When asked how she sees the virtual world shaping up in the next 5 to 10 years, Persis Trilling said that it will become the way many people communicate, as important as e-mail and more immediate. In terms of creation, the virtual world is cheaper but not less challenging. Equipment, like cameras and building tools, are built into the program, so there's no need to buy them. But the skill required to produce and build is the equivalent of the real world, and those with the right skills are raising the bar.

New World Opportunities

You may be a well-known company in the real world, but an unknown presence in the virtual world. Successfully establishing and marketing your business, brand, and services with a virtual-world presence through Second Life® can be achieved through a firm understanding of this online medium. As with any new venture, you are best equipped with knowledge of how this engine runs.

As immigrants who once came to the New World melting pot must have thought centuries ago, "Opportunity is what you make of it." Ask yourself what you want to make of your Second Life®. Then do it.

GETTING
STARTED

Profile

— ✕

2nd Life | Web | Interests | Picks | Classified | 1st Life | My Notes

Name: **Apple MacKay**

Photo:

Currently Online

Born:

6/27/2006

Account:
Resident
Payment Info Used

Partner: ⓘ ?

Nasus Dumart

Groups:
Counting Sheep
Diamond Deals Monthly Streams
Instructor
Macintosh Users
Molaskey's Pub

About:
(500 chars)

Molaskey's Pub Owner
Art gallery owner.
Apple Gallery
* * * Portrait by Wichi Studio Profile Enhancements * * *

Give item: Drop inventory item here.

☑ Show in search   ?

OK   Cancel

Release Keys

Local Chat   Click here to chat.

3.

The Essentials for Creating and Maintaining Your Second Life

Those who took the time to learn the Internet, for business or personal use, demonstrated the ease of global communication via e-mail, chat rooms, Web sites. and other features. Just as the Internet required a new skill set and plenty of practice, Second Life® requires some 3D skills and understanding in order to use it.

Millions of people have already experienced Second Life®, reporting mixed first impressions. These are the people who created a free account and a dorky avatar with an unpronounceable name. Then the unguided novices, or newbies, spend an hour trying to fix their avatar's look. After that, if they aren't being booted out of a place for indecent exposure or errantly teleporting somewhere without any hope of finding their way back, they walk into walls, eventually give up, and decide they have accomplished absolutely nothing. They haven't gone back because, not having the guidance or understanding of what Second Life® is all about, they just gave up.

Ease into your life in 3-D. Don't be disappointed if you don't learn it all at once. Practically no one does. Pace yourself. Find an experienced (and patient) host or mentor to help you, like a virtual-world personal trainer. Companies, such as IBM, Michelin, and Intel, and universities are equipping their employees and students with Second Life® skills through specially structured seminars and classes. Even with specialized classroom instruction, practical Second Life® training will come from guided first-hand experience.

Linden Lab and seasoned residents are fully aware of the learning curve. If you just type a question in open chat, someone will likely offer an answer, if not a full lesson. There are free tutorials and classes offered on Second Life® skills. An orientation course is an absolute necessity. Though it may seem easy for your avatar to walk, jump, fly, change appearance, teleport, dance, drive, chat, talk, and gesture in Second Life®, these activities are in fact acquired skills. Even the best trained new residents find themselves in freshman status during their first few weeks on the Second Life® campus.

Here is some practical advice for navigating your freshman weeks in Second Life®.

- Don't be afraid to make mistakes. The only real way to learn Second Life® is through trial and error.

- Take notes from the advice you receive, whenever it is offered.

- Learn how to use your keyboard and mouse for navigation before you try to change your appearance. Ask the people around you for help.

- Learn how to participate in chat, both in open space and with groups or one on one in private.

- Be sure to experience virtual-world travel. There are plenty of exceptionally replicated real-world places represented in Second Life®.

Before you know it, you'll be the one offering help to others. Books and demonstrations are informative, but the most effective path is to go into action. Take Steve Prentice's valuable advice: "Go, experiment and learn."

Getting started in Second Life® requires some new skills for navigating a 3D world. You need to develop a firm understanding of your avatar, the tools, and their capabilities. We have condensed the requirements into snippets of information, fully realizing that every person will have a unique experience beyond these basic functions.

Register with Linden Lab

Signing up for Second Life® is very easy. Go to their Web site, www.secondlife.com, and join. This requires that you provide Linden Lab with your real name, create a log-in password, and agree to the terms of service agreement. Linden Lab prides itself on the strict privacy they provide each Second Life® registrant.

Once you agree to the terms of service and provide valid identification and billing information, a notice is sent to your registered e-mail. You will be given notice that your account has been activated, along with instructions on how to download and install the Second Life® application.

Establish Your Contact Information

The key to maintaining your virtual-world presence while in the real world and vice versa is to dedicate an e-mail to your virtual-world existence, like (AvatarName)@gmail.com or (BusinessName)@yahoo.com. This is the key to harmoniously maintaining both lives. Whether it's gmail or Yahoo or any other preferred e-mail provider, the right contact information to provide the virtual world is whichever you will likely maintain with ease. When you are off-line, messages, group notices, and inventory notices will be sent to the e-mail address you provide upon registration. You will receive an e-mail for every notice given to your avatar. When you are part of several groups, the notices can add up. In addition, when someone sends you an instant message, it goes to your e-mail when you are logged off. You will not receive notices in e-mail when you are in-world, only when you are logged off.

If you prefer to use your existing e-mail address to receive your virtual-world notices, it's fine. Keeping your e-mails separate is just a strong suggestion.

Create Your Avatar

Before you can explore the world of Second Life®, you will create your avatar. An avatar is an incarnation of oneself in digital form. Your avatar is how the online world will identify you. To create the avatar, you must:

- Choose a name.

- Choose an appearance.

Choosing a Name

Before you create your virtual-world image, put some thought into your name. It is a decision with lasting impact. Your name is displayed over your avatar and will be seen wherever you go, just as you will be able to see the names of those around you.

You will answer to your (chosen) name in conversation, and it is how you will be known. The only way to create a new avatar name is to create an entirely new avatar.

You could consider a creative, cryptic version of your real name, a realistic business name, or something totally absurd. Whatever you choose, consider that others may have a hard time pronouncing it or typing it in conversation. Then you wind up with a nickname whether you like it or not.

Remember that your avatar will carry on for many years and may one day be transferable to other virtual worlds. Be confident in naming him or her. Each avatar has a first and last name. Your first name is entirely up to you. If you wish to have a double first name, you can put two names together, like "MaryAnn" or "JohnHenry" or "SensibleSue" without a space. It will count as one name but look like two.

Your surname is selected from a list of names provided by Linden Lab upon registering on the secondlife.com Web site. The surnames range from familiar names, like "Jameson," "McCullough," or "Darwin," to the absurd, like "Clawtooth," "Henhouse," or "Wrigglesworth." You may not choose world figures or celebrity names, names with foul language, or names with distasteful social provocation. You may, however, request a custom name through Linden Lab for a fee of $1,000 and $500 annual renewal.

No two avatars are ever the same, so there is no name duplication. If what you want is not available, you will be prompted to choose something else. Feel confident in knowing you will be one of a kind in Second Life®.

Choosing an Appearance

Once you select your avatar's name and provide a valid e-mail address, you are given the choice of a starter avatar with which you will enter the world. You have the option of being either a male or female despite your real-life gender. Once you enter the world, your avatar's appearance is completely modifiable, including gender, so it is a short-term commitment.

Using the general entry into Second Life®, you can choose from the following predesigned avatars:

- The girl or boy next door

- City chic

- Harajuku

- Cybergoth

- Furry

- Nightclub

In Second Life®, it is possible to be judged not by the color of your skin but by the content of your character. People choose how to represent themselves through their custom-made avatar. Those dealing with gender, racial, and disability barriers in real life may find Second Life® to be a more balanced playing field. In Second Life®, you may be judged on your virtual-world abilities, not your real-life disabilities. Taking people for how they choose to represent themselves can break the prejudices that come up in real life. In terms of equality, this lends an interesting perspective to conducting business.

Alternate Avatars

It is possible to maintain more than one avatar by creating a new account. It seems funny that a Second Life® avatar, your alternative identity from the real world, would actually need an alternative identity from the virtual world. But there are times when it might be a good idea.

We all have different communication situations for our lives. We have personal lives, a business life, organizational activities, and affiliations. Just as it makes sense to have separate e-mail accounts for certain situations, it can also make sense to have separate avatars.

Virtual-world character names will change as you go from one world to the other. Multiple avatar identities in the same world, however, can be considered a productive tool or a tool of deception. You may disclose your avatar's alternate identity in confidence to friends, or you may not. You decide what you are comfortable with.

It can be deceptive to interact with friends and associates without disclosing your alternate identity, though that option is yours.

Purists will say having one avatar keeps things genuine, and it can be an important quality of your character. Others will find a use for having an alternate, for multitasking, for managing a business account and a personal account, for social experimentation (having a male and female), or simply for starting over and recreating yourself for any reason.

Many people have several e-mail addresses, and, in most cases, e-mail accounts are changed, updated, abandoned, or closed because of intolerable spam. One main difference between an avatar and an e-mail is that your avatar has more control over the spam you receive. Although e-mailing is an effective and accepted way of group communication in Second Life®, when you are on an e-mail list, you receive unsolicited spam. In Second Life®, spam is generated through groups. If you are receiving pesky notices, you have the option to either leave the group spamming you or to turn off the option that allows spam to reach you. You don't need to create a new avatar because of the persistent and uncontrollable spam.

Welcome to Orientation Island in Second Life®!

If Second Life® is akin to the New World that America represented at the turn of the twentieth century, then Orientation Island is akin to Ellis Island. (They really should have a virtual Statue of Liberty there to greet newcomers.)

If you are entering Second Life® on a mission, perhaps looking to establish a virtual-world business, you have to be willing to take the time to learn how to function in this new world. When you log on to Second Life® for the first time, you are brought to Orientation Island. While on Orientation Island, you will learn basic skills, such as how to move, communicate, use the search tool, and modify your appearance.

There are friendly, knowledgeable volunteers on Orientation Island to help newcomers. You will also be provided with an automated tutorial. It is also possible to skip orientation and teleport right to a destination on the mainland, but the time you give to practicing on Orientation Island is worthwhile.

If you feel you haven't mastered the basic skills from Orientation Island before moving on to the rest of the world, don't worry. The seasoned residents throughout Second Life® are known for their friendly and helpful nature toward newbies. Don't be afraid to ask questions in open chat. Someone is likely to offer you help, understanding what it is like to be new to this multidimensional world.

There is a steep learning curve in Second Life®; that is, it's not easy to learn all at once. Even residents who use Second Life® regularly find there is always something new to learn. Think about it: No one mastered the Internet all at once because it is an evolving world. No one mastered real life as a baby; in fact, some would argue that it is nearly impossible to "master" real life at all. Everything comes with experience.

Orientation Island is just one general public area in which thousands of newcomers arrive each week. Once you're done orientating, you just teleport to a destination of your choice. A selection of destinations can be found by accessing search. If you're fortunate enough to know someone already established in Second Life®, you will have an easier time progressing.

There is also a volunteer group of Second Life® mentors whose goal is to help newbies acclimate to life in 3-D, providing positive experiences and direction for the tens of thousands of new arrivals each month.

Entry Portals Other Than Linden Lab's Orientation Island

Though the majority of newcomers to Second Life® will enter through Linden Lab's Orientation Island, it is not the only portal into Second Life®. Linden Lab has worked with major virtual-world participants, like NMC Virtual Worlds, Big Pond, The L Word, the NBA, CBS's *CSI:NY*, Warner Brothers' *Gossip Girl*, SL Netherlands, Mainland Brasil, The Azure Islands, STA Travel, and Dreamland, to name a few. These are all customized portals into Second Life®.

These select portals were established with the user experience in mind. They also help to disburse the average daily crowds of upward of 30,000 newcomers at any given time.

These unique entry points offer people familiar real-world surroundings, culture, and languages in the virtual world. By accessing Second Life® through a familiar portal, people are able to have a more positive start in the world by interacting with seasoned, like-minded Second Life® mentors.

The Second Life® Profile

When a person wants to know about someone else, profile information is accessed. With the exception of your name and the date you entered the world of Second Life®, your profile is customizable. Customizing your profile is not required, but if you're entering a social network, for business or pleasure, your impact on the world is better made with an informative, personalized profile.

To access your profile while logged in to Second Life®, click Edit on your toolbar, and a dropdown menu will appear. You can also do this by rightclicking an avatar (you or someone else) with your mouse, which will provide you with a pie menu. Select Profile.

Customized profiles offer a character description of an avatar by way of pictures and information offered. You can tell a lot about persons from their profiles, so make your impression on the world. Write something about your interests, projects, associations, and contact information. This section can be updated as frequently or infrequently as you want. If you keep up with it, a profile will reflect your disposition as often as it changes. Let your sense of humor or strictly business nature come through. Your profile can be and will be viewed. How you maintain it is entirely up to you.

Your profile consists of several tabs:

- 2nd Life

- Web

- Interests

- Picks

- Classified

- First Life

- Notes

The 2nd Life Tab

The 2nd Life tab is the front page of your profile. It contains the most information including your selected photo, the groups you are affiliated with, a section where you can type something about yourself, an area where others can drop an item into your inventory, your Second Life® born date (aka your rez date), your resident account status, your Second Life® partner (if any), and a check box with the option to be removed from the Second Life® search engine.

The Web Tab

You can load your traditional Web site into your Second Life® profile. When your profile is accessed, one of the tabs is Web info. You can load your Web site address into this section and activate load Web page option. When the Web section of your profile is opened, your Web site will be directly accessible. Though it is in a reduced window, it is a live connection to your site, not just a picture. You can scroll through the pages of the Web site without leaving Second Life®.

The Interests Tab

The Interests area of your profile offers a preselected range of interests, and you can add a checkmark next to the applicable ones. This begins with "I Want To:" and you check as many as apply in the areas of Build, Meet, Group, Sell, Explore, Be Hired, Buy, Hire. You may add a comment in the free-form area.

The next section is for Second Life® skills you have. They include textures, modeling, scripting, architecture event planning, and custom characters. Again, there is a section for a free-form comment.

Finally, you may list any language skills you have. This may humorously include typonese, a common real-time chat language that contains typos, but that is nonetheless readable or easily corrected. Aside from the humor, listing the real languages you speak and understand helps define your character.

The Picks Tab

There is a section of your profile where you may add your favorite places in SL™, including your own. This will include a picture, description, and landmark to your suggested favorite people and places. This is where you self-promote with suggested destinations.

The Classified Tab

You can easily place a Second Life® classified ad through your profile under the Classified tab. If you have property, items, or services to sell, you should place an ad to circulate throughout Second Life®. The classified ads generally run about L$50 a week, but for a prominently placed ad, you are advised to pay more. For instance, if you want to promote your sunglasses and accessories shop, and you are competing with a dozen other shops, you would be placed at the top of the search list results if you are the highest-paying advertiser. It's as easy as that. You just have to determine what you are willing to pay for the spot. Make sure you use the best keywords for people to find you; despite what you pay for your ad, your keywords will help direct the right customers to your shop.

The First Life Tab

In the First Life tab, you may tell others about the real you. This section offers a place to add your picture (or not) and a free-form writing area of up to 250 words. From here, you can refer people to a blog, Web site, or project you are working on in the real world. People keep their real life guarded until a trust is established in a relationship. Don't announce where you live or use real names, and expect others to do the same.

The Notes Tab

The Notes section is a very useful area to which only you are privy. You will interact with a lot of people in Second Life®, and it is impossible to keep track of everyone. When you meet someone, make a note of how you know that person by writing yourself a note in this section. Write whatever you want that will trigger a memory of how you know them. No one else will be able to see your note; it's for your reference only. This is an allowable cheat sheet or memory booster, a valuable tool in social networking. So, even after a span of time has passed, the next time you see that person, you can jog your memory by referring to your notes. It could be as simple as the date and place you met, who introduced you, a copy of relevant chat you had with them, or anything.

If you think someone's name is familiar, check the notes section of their profile for a message to yourself that you may have made. Demonstrating a good memory, of course, helps in any future conversations with the person and makes you look very sharp. I wish I had a real-life gadget with this feature!

Modifying Your Appearance

Although it is not necessary for the first few days or weeks after creating your avatar, one of the first things people like to do when they get in-world is change their appearance. This is a logical desire because your avatar should be as unique as your name, your personality, and your tastes—and your starter avatar may leave a lot to be desired. Luckily, Second Life® avatars are entirely customizable by their owners. Creativity is encouraged and appreciated, but certainly not required.

Often, people want to change just their clothes, hair, and accessories.

Clothing

To change your clothes, click your Inventory tab on the bottom menu bar. That pops open your Inventory window. Opened Inventory offers two tabs: All Items and Recent Items. During the time you are logged on, you will receive items in Recent Items, which automatically transfers to All Items when you are logged off.

Using the keyword "worn" will direct your Inventory to show you everything your avatar is wearing. That is useful information when you can't figure out if you are wearing an entire outfit or a mix of items. Then right-click on the items from that result, and Detach items as needed. Don't take something off to put something else on. Just replace pants with pants, shirt with a shirt, and so on. Otherwise, you'll experience a wardrobe "malfunction" in front of others. Better yet, be discreet and change your wardrobe in privacy.

To find a folder in your avatar's inventory, not just the recent items, make sure the All Items folder is highlighted. Use a keyword, like "hair" or "Molaskeys" or "Simone Design," and everything containing that word will result, including clothing, landmarks, and designer name items. Because you can't possibly remember every item by name, rename a file using a word you associate with it. For instance, I bought a beautiful dress for a special event. The designer named it "Elsbeth," a name that I couldn't associate with the dress, so I renamed it "ElsbethIrish Dress." With that name, I can find the dress faster when I need it. When I don't do that, I lose track of what I have. To date, I have nearly 9,000 items in my inventory, and I may have to just take the time and go through it all (not really!).

When you find the folder using a keyword, highlight it. Then highlight the keyword used to find it and erase it from the search bar. The folder will open, revealing what may include a complete outfit, not just what is worn or relevant to the exact keyword. Double-click and/or right-click to Wear. It sounds like a lot of steps, but, with practice, the process takes just a few seconds. You can rapidly change your outfit. The problem may be in selecting what to wear!

Appearance

To modify your avatar's physical condition, making it heavier, skinnier, or mixed proportioned unlike any other, you will need to Edit Your Appearance. Use your mouse to right-click on your avatar. That will bring up your Pie menu. The Pie menu options are Groups, Profile, Friends, Gestures, Take Off, and Appearance. To edit your avatar's physical features, click on Appearance. This will bring you into Appearance edit mode. You are given the options to custom-modify your shape, skin, hair, and eyes. This is also achieved by buying a ready-made shape and skin from one of the many boutiques run by Second Life® professionals.

The things you wear—clothes, skin, eyes, shirt, pants, shoes, jacket, gloves, undershirt, underpants, and skirt—are modifiable only with permission. Permissions to modify an object are established by its creator. Most—not all—items that are purchased are nonmodifiable to protect intellectual property rights. You may be able to edit the position of a garment, but most professionally made items universally fit avatars. Because you are given creative control, you may edit beyond the intended fit, but you may not be able to return to the original and that would be unfortunate.

The Search Function

Second Life® is an intranet with its own internal search engine. When a keyword search is performed using the Second Life® search engine, you will find results the same way you would on the Internet. The difference is that your internal search results are Second Life®–specific. When you click on a result, you are given a description of the business, group, avatar, or location, along with the option of teleporting to the location. As soon as you are registered with Second Life®, you can be searched. This is how you or your business or group will be found in Second Life®.

Camera/Your Point of View

Your viewer, the Second Life® application, functions as your eyes on the world, acting as your camera and your virtual-world point of view. You can also "cam" around while your avatar stays in place. You have the ability to zoom in, zoom out, get an aerial view, and other perspectives using your Option key, Command key, arrow keys, and mouse.

To experience the 3D world by looking around without moving your avatar, hold down the Option or Command key or right-click your mouse, holding it down while you move your mouse. Turn your view around and have a look at yourself. While holding down the Option key or right-click button, you can move your camera forward and backward. You can also hold down your Control (on the Mac) or Command button (on the PC) to move your camera view vertically. Play with these combinations to get familiar with your camera abilities. Double-click the Esc key or release the right-click to return to normal.

Your camera distance can be adjusted, giving you a nearly unlimited range to look around. This can be found by touching the Edit function found at the top of the screen on the menu bar. You will find preferences at the bottom of the drop-down menu. That will open a window where you will find a selection of settings, including Input and Camera. Adjust your camera distance as you wish. You can see things up very close or from an aerial view. Keep in mind, however, that so can everyone else.

Defining Your Mission, Forming a Group

With orientation and customized appearance out of the way, now you are ready to create your business presence. Social networking businesses are based on the relationships formed by groups. This is where you select the roles of the people in your group and build your clientele.

Forming a New Group

To form a new group, touch the Search tab at the bottom of your screen. This will open a new window. You will see tabs including All, Classifieds, Events, Showcase, Land Sales, Places, People, Groups, and Touch Groups. You have the option to search for a group using keywords, see what groups you already belong to, or create a new group.

When you touch on Create a New Group, it opens a new window, where you fill in the blanks with your group information. Make sure you get it right the first time. The group name cannot be edited once you confirm it. When you are ready, hit Apply. A prompt will notify you of the L$100 fee to form a group, and ask if you are "Really, really, REALLY sure you want to spend L$100 on this group." It also advises you that the group will be disbanded within 48 hours if no one else joins, leaving the name unusable for future use.

When you assign roles, the three options are Everyone, Officers, and Owners. Make sure you edit the titles. Give them a creative tag that members will proudly wear, not just "member," which is a generic name intended for creative input. Assign the proper roles to people. The role for everyone is for general membership. Officers are for your management, with restricted access to group privileges. Owners have full privileges.

Adding Members to Your Group

To add members, first open the group file. Touch the Communication tab at the bottom of your screen showing your groups and friends list, or you can right-click on your avatar to bring up your pie menu. You'll see Groups as an option. Touch it. Highlight the group name, which opens up the group profile. Touch the Info tab, and see the tab options at the top of group window: General, Members & Roles, Notices, Proposals, Land & L$. Touch Members & Roles, and you will see member names and the option to Invite New Person. That opens yet another window: Group Invitation with highlighted tab Open Person Chooser and touch it. That opens another smaller window: Choose Resident. Type the resident name: Nasus Dumart. When you double-click the correct name as it appears in the selection, you automatically go back to the Group Invitation window, where you can click the highlighted tab, Send Invitation. The Invitation will be automatically sent to the person or people on the list, who will get a pop-up on their screen to join or decline your invitation.

Take a look at the Roles; you can give a group tag for members to wear. Be creative. People like wearing witty group tags a lot more than just a generic Member. Also, assign general roles and officer roles, where someone has the authority to manage your group. Each role is distinguished by the titles you create, such as The Big Cheese, The Managing Cheese, and Member of the Cheese Platter.

In a social network, such as Second Life®, people seek others with similar interests. A person may log on to Second Life® to fulfill professional goals or to have a personal, recreational, intellectual, or social outlet. Joining a group or forming a group is not mandatory, but it is a powerful networking tool. Companies, organizations, educational institutions, and general interest groups thrive because of their group members.

Groups are an important part of your virtual-world identity. You can have a maximum of 25 group affiliations, and all of them are listed in your profile, which others can access. You can select a group name to be displayed over your avatar name, which appears in a text box that floats over each avatar. This is a great way to get the message out because your affiliation is as clearly projected to others as your name.

Ginsu ("Gene") Yoon, vice president of business affairs with Linden Lab, explained why groups are limited to 25 per avatar:

> We realize that this issue is important to Residents, especially Residents who utilize groups to run their businesses. Group-related queries and operations are currently among the most complex of our database operations that happen on the grid. The more groups Residents can join, the more complex these queries become—there are more groups, more group-to-agent relationships, and more roles. Because of this, increasing the group limit could affect the performance of the grid, so it's something we need to consider very carefully before moving ahead. While there's a significant interest in increasing the capacity to join groups, we won't be able to put forward a timeline for when this may happen until the potential technical issues have been fully considered. We are evaluating the impact on the back end systems of making such an increase and that we'll let everyone know if we can't offer the increase, given the potential negative impact on performance.

The General Section of Your Group Profile

In this section you will find the group insignia, founder name, group charter, owners, officers, members, active title, and group preferences. The group insignia is a snapshot or photograph that is used to visually identify the group. The group insignia is the group logo and appears with each notice sent to members.

The group insignia can be a simple Second Life® snapshot, dropped onto the blank insignia space, or it can be an elaborate logo, perhaps created in Photoshop or another program. The Group Charter is a mission statement about the group. This is a free-form writing area where you succinctly explain your goals for the group.

Money Matters

Method of Payment

You can sell items through a vending system, where avatars in Second Life® click-to-pay for items, and the items are automatically delivered to their inventory upon purchase. This method accepts Linden dollars only.

Payment for services has to be established in a service agreement. For small projects, services are compensated with Linden dollars. For more in-depth, professional services, a contract between parties is established and invoices are settled with real currency.

Linden Lab upholds Second Life® residents' privacy, and therefore methods of payment are kept to the in-world currency. For transactions other than $L payment, links to PayPal or credit-card-accepting Web sites are used. Products and services can be paid for by clicking and paying, automatically transferring from the purchaser's account to the seller's account.

Cash Flow Statements and Income Statements

Your transaction history, including payments, income, gifts, tips, and other transactions, can be found by logging in to http://secondlife.com using your avatar name and password.

You will need to address income tax questions with an accountant. In the United States, you must claim income earned over $600. Businesses must meet quarterly tax payments. All Second Life® income statements can be found online by accessing your account. In addition to your bank statements, you will have the records necessary to verify your income. Consult an accountant for professional advice on your earnings and business investments.

Funds Request

Your account balance is displayed in the upper right-hand corner of your screen at all times. You can request funds at anytime through your client option, drawing funds from the account established upon registering. Deposits take 24 to 28 hours to be processed into your real-life account.

Your fund request is processed through the LindeX, which converts Linden dollars to real-world currency. Linden Lab fees associated with withdrawing your funds are automatically calculated into the transaction.

Gene Yoon of Linden Lab explains how the Linden Commerce works, producing U.S. dollars:

> L$ are used to pay for virtual goods and services in Second Life®, and can be bought and sold for USD on the LindeX; there are also a number of third-party exchanges that Residents can choose to use. Residents retain the Intellectual Property (IP) rights to their creations in Second Life®, which enables them to monetize the content they create. For example, if I create a virtual object, I own the rights to that design and can sell it to you for L$ (which you've purchased for USD). I can then take the L$ I've

earned and sell them on the LindeX for USD. Currently, Residents can buy and sell L$ on the LindeX only for USD, but there are exchanges operated by third parties (i.e., not Linden Lab) that may allow Residents to buy and sell L$ for pounds sterling, for example.

Cost of Development

Basic membership to Second Life® is free. However, premium membership allows you to own land. When you own virtual land, equivalent to owning a Web domain, you pay a monthly maintenance fee to Linden Lab. The monthly rates vary according to the amount of virtual land you own. At the time of writing, the following rates applied:

Size	Area (m²)	Cost (U.S. $)
$\frac{1}{128}$ Region	512	5
$\frac{1}{64}$ Region	1,024	8
$\frac{1}{32}$ Region	2,048	15
$\frac{1}{16}$ Region	4,096	25
$\frac{1}{8}$ Region	8,192	40
$\frac{1}{4}$ Region	16,384²	75
$\frac{1}{2}$ Region	32,768	125
Entire Region	65,536	195
Private Island	65,536	295

Linden Lab offers a 50% discount to verified real-world educators and academic institutions (e.g., universities and schools) or 501(c)3 nonprofit organizations that will be using the regions to support their organization's official work.

Once you are a Resident and have established your monthly payment, your next cost of development will be supplies and labor, then marketing and advertising, and finally your staff.

Create Your Business!

Now that you have the basics of Second Life® down, you are ready to create your business plan. But take time to explore the world first. Search for competitors and possible collaborators. Visit their buildings, islands, and see whether you can introduce yourself to some potential allies. Invite people to join your group, build relationships, and, above all, have fun doing it!

4.

Your Virtual Real Estate

One of the most exciting ways to position yourself and your business in Second Life® is to invest in real estate. Just as in real life, your real estate provides a destination for people seeking your product or service. By investing in real estate you can:

- Have a searchable location.

- Create an expression of your brand, product, or service that has an impact.

- Offer people a place to go when you're offline.

- Provide important information about your product or service.

- Hold demonstrations.

- Host special events.

- Generate an income by renting parcels of your land.

You have the choice of mainland or island property. Mainland property is a continuous link of regions. Islands are independent of the mainland. Many companies and business-minded individuals invest in island property to develop their brand in Second Life®. Because each region or island runs on a single server, by buying an island a company or individual rents an entire virtual-world server from Linden Lab (LL™).

Although you can own property on someone else's land, part of your real estate agreement might include paying the tier, paying fees to Linden Lab for maintaining the server, and paying for the use of real estate tools for modifying the topography. Landowners have total control over every aspect of their property's look and feel by using their estate tools.

Others prefer to rent and pay the owner of the island a monthly or weekly fee in Linden dollars. Many buildings on rental properties are prefabricated; you just move your product into them and design the interior placement. Landowners will give you the option of custom-building or placing your own prefabricated building on the land. Prefabricated buildings are available for sale throughout Second Life® and can be easily kept in inventory and dropped onto land where you have permission to place items.

Make sure you stay well within your prim limits for the parcel of land you're on. Prims will be randomly returned to their rightful owner when pressed to the limit. This can be complicated and frustrating if someone innocently places an item on your prim-heavy land only to have something else disappear to make room for it. That is why many landowners restrict others from placing additional items on their land. These restrictions are in the best interest of everyone's items, so that things don't randomly disappear.

Owning Versus Renting Your Real Estate

The first decision you will need to make is whether you want to rent or own your real estate. There are benefits and disadvantages to both, and it is important that you resolve your vision for your property with the practicalities of development, your capabilities, and your privacy needs.

Owning

Second Life® real estate is nothing more than a 3D virtual-world domain. When you buy an island, Linden Lab provides the hardware and maintenance. It is up to you to develop your virtual land or hire someone to develop it for you. Either way, you own a Second Life® address. You pay Linden Lab every month for the service to maintain the server, and the rates are determined by the amount of land you own.

Islands are 65,536 square meters in size, with an allowance of 15,000 prims. You can own as many islands as you'd like and even have your islands located near one another. Islands can be set as public or private, and they can be divided into parcels for sale or rent.

You can also buy and develop property on a mainland region. The mainland is a part of the main cluster of regions connected to one another. The property can vary in size from 512 square meters to 65,536 square meters, with prim allowances from 117 to 15,000. Mainland regions may provide random traffic to your site, while offering a true sampling of the local Second Life® culture. Each parcel has its own monetary value set by the owners. What you do with your land is up to you.

Creating a Scene

John Mahon is a native of Dublin, Ireland. When he first entered Second Life® in 2005, he instinctively knew Second Life® "needed an anchor," a social gathering spot, such as a proper Irish pub. So he built The Blarney Stone Pub in Second Life®. It became so crowded on the mainland that he bought an island to relocate it. But the sim John bought was too big for just a bar, and it had to be put into context with its surroundings. That's when the idea of building a neighborhood happened. Because The Blarney Stone was built in Second Life® on the inspiration of an actual Dublin pub, the neighborhood that would fill the sim would naturally be Dublin, SL™ (DublinSL.com), one of the all-time most popular places in Second Life®.

Dublin has many reasons for attracting people from all over the world. There's the famous St. James Gate at the Guinness Brewery, Trinity College, beautiful architecture, friendly people, and thriving businesses. Dublin in Second Life® became such a good representation of the city of Dublin, Ireland, John began to receive inquiries to rent the buildings he owns, because "the rent is more affordable than in real life." As (Irish) luck would have it, the first to take up residence in Dublin, SL™ was the Irish public relations firm, Think House. Not only do they support Dublin SL™ with healthy media coverage, but they also chose the most valuable real estate in Dublin SL™, across from The Blarney Stone Pub.

Cons

- At the time of writing, the going rate for an island in Second Life® is $1,000, plus a monthly maintenance fee of $295 ($3,540 annually). This is for a new island custom-ordered through Linden Lab. Islands are also for sale from previous owners at various rates. In addition to the annual cost of an island, you must consider the purchase price of the island along with the costs of contractors, materials, and entertainment. Though the total is a modest investment for large marketing departments, it is a steep investment for many, especially when the return may not come as fast as you need it.

- Mainland parcels may not perform as well as islands. Mainland parcels have more lag and are more public than islands. (Lag is when the interactive performance is slow, causing a disappointing experience for visitors.)

- Mainland properties are subject to high turnover. You do not have say in who moves in around you, and you could have conflict with them or their clientele.

- If your neighbor's land is script-heavy, where animations cause slow performance, sim performance decreases. It is harder to move an avatar around and access links, type-chat, and search inventory. Your clients will therefore not have as positive an experience as you would like.

- A stipend is no longer offered to residents younger than those "born" on June 6, 2006. Linden Lab offered residents an incentive of up to L$400 a week for buying land and contributing to the development of Second Life®.

- Mainland property resale value fluctuates between 5 and 45–50 a square meter.

Pros

- You have creative control. You may transform the terrain, use up to 15,000 primitives (objects), choose your media stream and music, and establish privacy settings on land and in skyboxes. You can create the look you want based on your goals.

- Islands are separated from the mainland, so lag is less of an issue. Islands usually offer better overall sim performance.

- Landowners also have the ability to draw an income from rent.

- Real estate is one of the most profitable areas of business in Second Life®.

- To those who created their Second Life® account prior to June 6, 2006, and who upgrade to a premium account, which allows you to become a landowner, Linden Lab pays a weekly stipend ranging from L$50 to L$400. It's sort of like the game of Monopoly, where those landing on your property pay you rent *and* you get $200 for passing Go.

- As long as the monthly fee is maintained, the land is yours forever. It can even be bequeathed to someone in the event of your death.

- As in real life, Second Life® real estate has value, and it can be an investment. You can always sell your land (usually at a profit) if you no longer want it. Also, if you follow the market in Second Life®, you can strategically buy and sell, or you can flip real estate quickly, making a relatively fast return on investment. Because these are the early stages of Second Life®, years from now you may thank yourself for getting a piece of land now while it is affordable and available.

Renting

If you're taking a wait-and-see approach or if you want to get started sooner rather than later without a big commitment, you may be more comfortable renting space that's ready to move into. Rent is paid in Linden dollars to the landowner either as a weekly, monthly, or quarterly term of agreement and is usually enticingly affordable.

Cons

- You don't own the land; therefore you cannot sell it. Just as in real life, you can rent property for as long as you pay the rent. The owner makes a profit from your rent and the eventual sale of the property.

- You are also restricted to the design aspects and land permissions as set by the owner. If an owner created a neighborhood using ultramodern design, you may not be able to use your medieval décor as you may have wanted.

- Land permissions restrict the placement of items onto the land other than by the owner. Waiting for the owner to be available to you to place or edit the placement of objects could be a waste of valuable time.

Pros

- Plenty of places are available for rent that will suit your needs, whatever they are. Your choices can range from medieval to ultramodern, from fantasy to realistic, from abstract to traditional. You have many choices.

- If you move in to a prebuilt area, you don't have to develop your own site. That is a huge benefit for people without 3D building skills or the time or desire to learn them. Prebuilt neighborhoods make establishing your Second Life® presence easy. You can focus more on your business in Second Life® than on the building, freeing you to hit the ground running.

- Even if you don't own land in Second Life®, you can still have a Second Life® address. Have parties, invite friends, show off your shop, display your product/service/brand, provide links to your Web site, and get your Second Life® bearings.

- You don't pay a monthly fee to Linden Lab, just your rent, in Linden dollars, to your landlord or landlady.

The Ideal Neighborhood

Silicon Island in Second Life® is home to many corporate offices. Silicon Island owner, SL™-Liam Kanno, keeps an office there for his company, The V3 Group, and rents out the other buildings to interested and serious real-life companies while they get their virtual-world bearings. His neighborhood is designed as an ultramodern corporate park, connecting offices with sidewalks lined with plants. He has a directory so that visitors can stroll the campus and explore. The companies there tend to be cutting-edge and online media companies that work well as neighbors. The Barak Obama Presidential Campaign office even made a home on Silicon Island, using new media to raise political awareness. Everyone is quietly at work as random visitors come and go.

The companies that rent property on Silicon Island can very well afford to have their own island and corporate park, but they determine their uses for Second Life® and their real estate needs. For them, being established in Second Life® on Silicon Island in a beautifully designed office park with like-minded professionals is just what they want.

- Eye-catching posters and billboards with a link to a Web site make sense in a low-prim situation, because they only use one to five prims and offer a wealth of information. Renting a small space can be inexpensive and effective.

- Renting has no strings attached: no life-long commitment, no legalities. Just find a place, contact the owner, pay the rent as agreed, and move in. If you'd like to move on, you can take your things and go without even a moving truck.

- Many prebuilt buildings exist in a community neighborhood. Renting in a neighborhood with other professionals and steady traffic can be a great way of networking.

Developing Real Estate

If you choose to purchase property, you have the ability to develop it as you wish. In Second Life®, many things are possible because you are not bound by the same confines as the real world. You have a blank canvas in which to construct a creative, functional, and impressionable destination, whatever that may be. Decide whether you want something abstract or traditional. Is it going to push the boundaries of virtual-world experience or embrace a more realistic environment? The structure is only part of the establishment; the details and interaction complete the build.

To build your real estate, you will need to map out a development plan, either by yourself or with a builder (you can do a search for builders, and select someone you think will meet your needs). Here are some things to keep in mind as you create your plan.

- What is the main function of the island: community gatherings, business meetings, social events, private meetings?

- What environment do you want to have? You may choose a snowy landscape, forest, city, beach, or other setting.

- What type of structures do you want: tree houses, yachts, cabins, teepees, office building, nightclub?

- Do you want a central courtyard branching outward or a walkway around the circumference?

- Do you want the style to be realistic, abstract, historic, traditional, or ultramodern?

No matter what you decide, having an idea before you or your builder put the time and effort into it helps in the timely development of your land. Keep in mind that everything is modifiable and not set in stone. If you decide to change anything about your development plan, such as a switch from cityscape to peaceful forest office environment, it can be done.

Topography

When you purchase land from Linden Labs, you choose a basic topography, or the physical features of a region. Before you buy, you must decide what kind of land suits your purposes. Topography is generally modifiable. For instance, if your land has a hilly region, you can modify the height and span of the hills. If you have waterfront property, you can modify the sand and water however you want. You can flatten land for buildings or raise it for effect. You cannot, however, fully transform a snowy region into a beach area or a hilly region to flat lands. A skybox (a structure that is far up in the air) is attractive for some purposes. Skyboxes require teleportation into and out of them, and they can be hard to find randomly. On the other hand, having a skybox offers a level of privacy that can be useful for private conversations and meetings.

Primitives (Prims)

All 3D building in Second Life® begins with primitives, or prims. Primitives are basic 3D shapes, like cubes, cones, and cylinders. Primitives can be resized, reshaped, hollowed out, and otherwise modified into the form you need. To make a chair, for instance, you begin with a box, then you modify it to the basic shape. Then, for an authentic look, you may want to add spindles, each of which may be one prim.

Actually, this is an inefficient use of prims. You are permitted a certain number of prims to use on a sim (the common term for simulator, or the hardware that generates the virtual world). If the sim reaches the allowable maximum of prims, it disallows the placement of any other objects. Many people get carried away with prims when building in 3D. Making a simple chair in as many as 30 pieces is not practical. When you have limited prim use, each prim counts. You'd be far better off with a three-prim chair than with a 30-prim chair. There are efficient ways of building, using minimal prims and techniques.

When a prim is created, it is given X, Y, and Z factors: height, width, and depth. These geometric values are the very foundation of a 3D world. It's what offers the depth of field for moving your avatar around.

Building in 3D requires the skill to maneuver your camera while building. To start, go into Edit mode, touch Create, and select a shape—a cube, cone, cylinder. Then place that shape on the ground. Next, size, shape, and rotate the object as desired, using the Second Life® edit tools found in your Edit window from the toolbar. Create as if you were molding clay, creating, designing, and transforming however you see fit. It's not easy. Not everyone is a builder, but if you try your hand at it, you'll appreciate a skilled 3D builder even more.

Textures

Textures are the visual makeup on primitives or objects. A texture can be used like wallpaper, a paint job, shingles, siding, banners, or posters. It can be anything you can imagine. If you build a house and want it to have a weathered cedar shake appearance, you would texture the exterior wall with an image of a weathered cedar shake, then modify its scale to fit the building so that it is a realistic 3D object. Inside the building, if you want, say, splintered floorboards for authenticity, simply apply that texture to the floor prim and—voila!—splintered floorboards.

Textures can be created from photographic images or software programs, or they may be purchased from a texture shop in Second Life®. Textures in Second Life® need to be in the form of a graphic file in either .TGA (targa) or .BMP (bitmap) format, set to 24-bit color depth.

Scripting

Scripts give objects an *interactive ability* and are a great and powerful tool in a 3D interactive world. The scripting language in Second Life® is understandable to a degree, but the most apt skilled scripters are in demand for creating the more impressive, interactive objects. Scripts are not easy, if you don't understand computer coding, but they are necessary to the virtual-world experience. Entire manuals are written on the subject, and unfortunately it is beyond the scope of this book.

Becoming a Second Life® Real Estate Mogul

If you follow the market in Second Life®, you can strategically buy and sell or flip real estate quickly, making a relatively fast return on investment. Many people have caught the real estate bug in Second Life®; that is, they buy and sell real estate in Second Life® as a money-making hobby. They understand the market, watching auctions and sales every day of every week and making offers on land for purchase. Then, they either develop it for renting or sell it during a seller's market, that is, when the sell price is greater than the purchase price and there's demand for land. They do it over and over again. It becomes a business they love.

Finding neighborhoods where you can rent out space is a great idea. Owning the neighborhood may prove to be better, depending on your commitment to developing Second Life®. Savvy virtual-world real estate moguls are developing entire neighborhoods and cities at an amazing rate, to the delight of ready-to-move-in renters.

Here are some of the practicalities of becoming a real estate mogul.

Developing

- Real estate moguls hire a team of skilled, reliable builders as needed.

- Developing land can be done as quickly as 3 to 30 days, depending on the scope of the work.

- The more unique and practical features and interesting architecture a land has, the more valuable it is.

- Rather than just developing a plot of land, consider a neighborhood. You could create and manage several rental properties with like-minded professionals or residents.

Buying and Selling

- You can view land for sale while logged in to SL™ by touching the Map tab at the bottom of your screen. Any land for sale around you will appear in yellow. You can access all available land by touching the Search tab at the bottom of your screen and then touching the Land Sales category.

- You must upgrade your Second Life® membership from basic to premium, at a rate of $9.95 a month, to become a landowner.

- As long as you are a Premium Second Life® resident with enough Linden dollars in your account, you can simply buy the available land by pointing and clicking.

- Land can also be purchased by auction on the Second Life® Web site or by accessing the search engine in Second Life®.

- The more traffic you are able to generate on your land, the more valuable it is. Generating traffic is achieved with special events.

- You don't need high-tech building skills to be successful in real estate, but you will need a firm understanding of Second Life® communities and marketplace.

Flipping

- Buy low, sell high. It's the same game in Second Life®.

- You can find, at reasonable rates, dozens of properties, which you can develop and sell at a very fast pace.

- Many people are generating an income from flipping real estate.

- Flipping real estate can cause inflation. Property that used to cost L$5,000 is now going for L$50,000 or more. The SL™ community is very sensitive to this practice.

Real Estate Rentals and Sales, with a Smile

In 2004, SL™-Alliez Mysterio, an out-of-work legislative assistant, bought a sim in Second Life® and established a residence. She enjoyed SL™ real estate so much that she offered quality Second Life® land for rent, which people would refer to as their second home. Alliez took care of her customers, offering to customize their land and helping them get familiar with Second Life®. She made sure each parcel of land she rented was spaced far enough apart so that conversations from neighbors would not be seen in chat. Her hospitality became legendary, and many more came to her for a peaceful, private plot of virtual land to call their own. The land soon paid for itself and made a profit, so Alliez bought more sims—in fact, 96 of them to date, servicing about 900 renters. She makes a very good living renting Second Life® real estate, but she earns every dollar. Alliez makes herself available to her clients about 80 hours a week with several trusted managers on call.

- Buying real estate and developing it for rental income is far more agreeable with the community.

Buying and selling virtual-world real estate is similar to real-world real estate, with some notable differences:

In the real world, buying and selling real estate requires a tremendous amount of:

- Time spent searching the listings, driving place to place, scheduling a tour of the property

- Money—hundreds of thousands (and into the millions, too) of dollars— exchanged in the preparation to sell, buy, and fix up real estate

- Legal expenses

- Home inspections

- Credit checks

- Effort

In the virtual world, real estate transactions take a fraction of the time and money. There are no legal documents, home inspections, or credit checks. You just buy and sell at will. The effort put into the virtual-world market is often rewarded with a profit. Profits made from dealing Second Life® real estate range from a hundred dollars to several hundred thousand dollars. Though virtual-world real estate is a fraction of the real-world real estate market profit, it is at least a profit for your time and effort, and for many it is enjoyable.

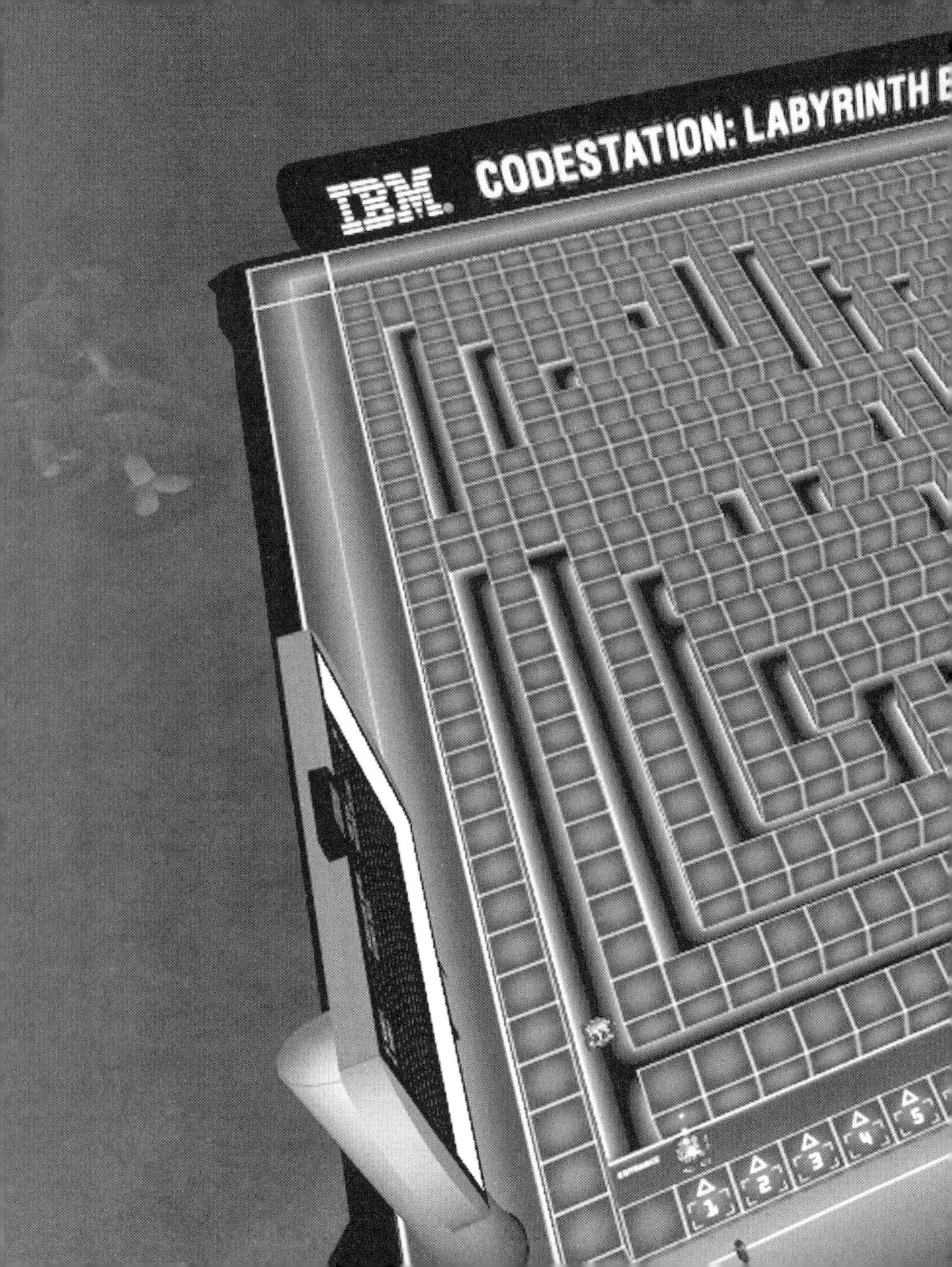
IBM.
CODESTATION: LABYRINTH

5.

Creating a Business Plan

As the previous chapters have shown, businesses of every shape and size are establishing themselves in the virtual world. The divide between in-world and real-world businesses are blurring as each supports the other: Real-world organizations are creating virtual presences, virtual businesses are expanding into the real world, and some virtual businesses can exist only in-world.

Because the virtual world is still an emerging platform on which to build a business, organizations large and small will face the similar opportunities and challenges. Second Life® is, above all, a social network. The underlying purpose is for people to interact. It is not a Web site that you can build and expect people to arbitrarily visit and find their way around. Second Life® requires your attention. Businesses, large and small, cannot rely on Second Life® or Linden Lab® to directly sell products to consumers. Rather, Second Life® is a platform for unique promotions, branding, interaction with the consumer, global conferencing, and collaborative projects. Second Life® businesses must engage with the virtual world, and it is up to business owners to figure out how to go about it.

People from all walks of life with unique ideas can consider Second Life® fertile ground for long-term business success. And like all businesses, setting off on the right foot is essential. Rather than doing business haphazardly, the guidance provided by a thoughtful and well crafted business plan can increase your profit and assist you in making decisions as you grow.

To establish your professional presence in Second Life®, you will need to make several long-term and some short-term decisions. *If you fail to plan, you plan to fail.* Your virtual-world business, though still considered a nontraditional business, can only benefit from traditional business planning. The Small Business Administration (SBA) recommends that you create a business plan whether or not you are seeking additional funding. By creating a business plan, you force yourself to think through your goals and the market in which you want to do business. It helps identify the potential and the risks, which will help you make sound decisions. The three main issues addressed by the business plan are:

1. The role(s) of the owner(s)

2. The proposed business and its market

3. The financial requirements and projections

Creating *Your* Plan

The Grid is a special section of the Second Life® Web site that provides updated facts that you may need to establish a business plan. It is an official source of Second Life® business information, such as growth charts, financial statistics, available real estate, and professional services. As you proceed through this section, remember that business plans are not a one-size-fits-all road map. They represent the core methods for how to think through the process of starting, running, and growing a business. Therefore, customize the business plan to suit your needs.

You may be nurturing a brilliant idea, or maybe have already started making money from a good idea. Either way, your business plan can be a way of getting organized for the long haul. While that rush of getting a good idea going can start us out, to grow, you need to devise a strategy. If it's time to take your start-up to the next level, your initial moves are crucial. Your goals and strategy take you there. It is never too late to plan.

Even if you are with a large corporation, and you see how Second Life® can add value to your company, you will need to present your ideas to management. Going through the steps of preparing a business plan can make sure you have covered all the bases.

Also, a business plan is an organizational tool that works best in writing. Although individuals may think they can keep it in their heads and not compile a written plan, when you involve others in the development of your business, you may need to present a concrete overview to bring them into the loop and establish how they fit into the picture. You will need to refer to it regularly, to remember your goals, and to gauge your progress.

Having a written business plan doesn't mean it doesn't change. Unexpected things happen that affect your strategy. You could start out with a simple plan to make and sell an item in the virtual world while having a good time, as long as it doesn't interfere with your real-life schedule. But if your product has potential and adds an additional stream of income, I doubt you will stick to your simple plan and leave it at that. You are likely to change your goals from simply experimenting in the virtual world to actually making something of it. You may find your virtual business suddenly becomes quite real. Be ready to go with that flow.

The Components of a Business Plan

An effective business plan has eight parts:

1. Business Description

2. The Market

3. Pricing and Sales Strategies

4. Virtual World Development and Production

5. Advertising and Public Relations

6. Business Management

7. Financial and Legal Considerations

8. Exit Strategy

1. Business Description

Of the many styles of being active in a Second Life® business, the three most common are the grassroots establishment, the entrepreneur, and the corporate department. Identify your level of participation and commitment, and communicate that in your business plan.

1. *The Grassroots Group Establishment.* A grassroots establishment consists of a group of people who contribute ideas and blocks of time while distributing responsibilities according to individual skills and interests. Members of this style of business have real-life jobs and manage their Second Life® venture on a part-time basis for the pure enjoyment of it. The Molaskey Group falls into this category.

2. *The Entrepreneur.* Second Life® entrepreneurs are out to build a full-time business in Second Life®. Many of them start out solo and then hire additional employees as their businesses grow. Simone Stern independently started Simone Design in 2004. She now earns more than $200,000 a year from her virtual-world fashion retail business, and she has extended her staff to one manager and several building contractors.

3. *The Corporate Department.* Real-world companies set up shop in Second Life® for many reasons, including branding, selling products, communication, and educational visual displays. But they soon find that establishing a viable and worthwhile virtual-world presence requires at least one person dedicated to the project. That person would develop and manage a virtual-world presence, in much the same way a Web developer is dedicated to a Web site.

Overview of Industry

When giving an overview of your industry in a Second Life® business plan, you will have to do so in two terms: real life and Second Life®. Many businesses fuse the real world with the virtual world. Your Second Life® business does not need to offer just virtual-world goods. Many are finding Second Life® a viable market for real-world goods and services. Coldwell Banker, for instance, has used virtual abilities to feature real-life properties. Manpower, the human resourcing company, is testing Second Life® for placing people in both real-life jobs and Second Life® jobs; this is known as creating a mixed reality. So you will need two distinct descriptions of the industry you are in, plus a third description of how the real world and virtual world intertwine in your business.

"Industry" is simply a category of viable business. It could be aerospace industry, automotive industry, biotechnology industry, construction industry, energy industry, entertainment industry, financial services industry, hospitality industry, information technology industry, transportation industry, and so on. In your business plan, describe the industry, specifying the area that you are looking to develop.

Let's say you are a manager in the entertainment industry. In the real world, the entertainment industry is a vast industry of artists, writers, technicians, and other creative people who collaborate to produce live and recorded performances. Perhaps you have an agency that manages several artists. You are responsible for publicity, scheduling, and negotiating fees and contract terms. In your business plan, you could discuss the amount of real-world money your industry generates, the number of people working together, and your specific goals.

Then consider the requirements that are unique to the virtual world.

Producing a show in the virtual world involves not only the same tasks as in the real world, but also technical ability to stream audio and video. The industry in which you work in the real world may have separate responsibilities, such as management and technical operation, but in the virtual world those responsibilities merge. Technical operators may find that they have to manage, and managers may find they have to perform technical duties.

The scale of your industry in Second Life® may be very different from that of your industry in real life. Even though the virtual world is experiencing an industrial revolution and Second Life® is seeing rapid growth, compared to other industries, it is still in a development stage. On the other hand, some industries are bigger in the virtual world than in the real world, due to specific opportunities like 3D building and development, avatar design, virtual-world haute couture, and other factors.

If your industry has not yet tapped into the virtual world, you may be at both an advantage and disadvantage in being the first to do so. Getting in early gives you the advantage of mastering the virtual world before the millions that are likely to follow. You can experiment and learn from blunders without major consequences. On the other side, getting in early and learning as you go means you will make mistakes, but those experiences lead to the refinement of the virtual world for years to come.

Mixed Reality

Describing your industry in terms of mixed reality ties it all together. For instance, a musician may perform in both real life and Second Life® in venues produced simultaneously for both audiences. To achieve this, they have to coordinate real-world and virtual-world schedules, agree to the terms of the performance, and address all other factors, such as publicity and technical operation. Then they perform to the delight of both audiences. They are being paid a fee for the Second Life® performance and from the ticket sales of the real-life audience.

Those in other industries, such as architecture, find it more difficult to make use of mixed reality. In the real world, an architect may design a site for a client, draw plans for the builder, and even implement them into a digital presentation. In Second Life®, an architect will plan and build a site, using the precision of the geometric grid of the 3D world, and then invite world visitors to enjoy the site. As a mixed reality, blending both the real world and the virtual world, the architect can build a scale model of a real site and invite clients to experience it prior to building it in real life. The architect may be in New York, and his clients may be in Chicago. The clients can convene in Second Life® and plan the layout, design, colors, and other details of the site before it goes to the builder. Delivering a virtual presentation takes time and precision up front, but it actually may save time and money overall.

In Second Life®, you have the opportunity to develop a career in an area completely independent of your real-life career. The Second Life® experience can be very fulfilling to those who are working, for instance, as accounting office managers in the real world but who want to express themselves creatively or socially through, say, landscape design or running a nightclub.

Description of Your Company

If someone casually asks you about your company, are you able to describe it to them in one simple statement? This sound bite is what you're perfecting in your business plan.

A statement about the company you are developing helps you define your mission and goals down the road. But it is the most helpful when communicating your purpose to bankers, vendors, suppliers, and customers.

In Second Life®, it is not uncommon to discuss a business using vocabulary such as "avatars," "skins," "furries," "prims," "stream," or even "gore," but to talk about it in the real world, in a business manner, may be difficult. Very often, people will premise a description of their virtual-world company with a deep breath and short, familiar words, so as not to overwhelm the person with whom they are speaking. You could also include a brief glossary. With any luck, the person will be curious about the virtual world and fascinated with your business.

When you are describing your virtual-world business to someone who is mostly unaware of the emerging market of the virtual world, you will be asked many questions. Be prepared for them. This type of audience will need an overview as well as the details. In your business plan, you might want to summarize the history of the virtual world, as described earlier in this book, and offer a sense of its future, as we describe at the end of the book.

Mission Statement

Start your company description with your mission statement. Your mission statement should communicate a clear statement of purpose. Companies without a simple, clear description can easily go off track. Although you may have a clear idea of your company's purpose and function, describing it succinctly on paper will help you stay focused and communicate that focus to others. As an example, here is the mission statement from The Molaskey Pub Group.

> Molaskey's Pub is committed to providing a quality destination for live music, competitive gaming, and social events for an overall positive virtual world entertainment experience.

In this mission statement, everything the business does is put into one sentence. The statement communicates what product and service the business provides, what it is about, and what its customers can expect from their experience at the place of business. The mission statement sets the operating parameters for the business and gives it a way to gauge success. In the case of Molaskey's Pub, the owners know that if people are enjoying themselves, they are on the right track. (In fact, we know we are achieving our mission because Molaskey's Pub visitors often comment on how comfortable they are at our place, comparing it to favorite real-life Irish pubs.)

Description of Products and Services

In this part of the business plan, you will need to be specific about your product or service. Highlight what makes your product special or what makes your services stand out from the competition's.

Describing your products and services gives you the opportunity to further define your purpose by highlighting what you actually do to achieve your mission. Although you may be able to do multiple jobs, describe your essential products and/or services. For instance, if your business is creating virtual beach content, such as surfboards and bathing suits, and you have other skills, such as sand castle making and instruction, don't get sidetracked with all that you are able to do. Focus on the key aspects of your business. At the Molaskey Group, Apple MacKay built the pub. He built every wall, seat, and stage. He built the ceiling, floor, fireplace, DJ booth with spinning turntable, the bar, and even the beer tap. But our product is the pub itself. In our business plan, we describe our product.

> The pub is a high-quality 3-D structure that is visually pleasing, tastefully decorated, and offers fun interactions and great events that make Molaskey's Pub a popular Second Life® destination.

Service

Describing what you do and how you do it will instill confidence in investors and offer employees a road map. If you ever wonder whether you're still on track, you can refer to this simple description. For example, if customers can go to your store in Second Life® and interact with your representatives in a very personalized manner, you will want to communicate that your business takes pride in its customer service and personal attention.

Here is what we do at The Pub.

> Each week at The Pub, we have a schedule of events that includes an average of five to ten hours of live music, a two-hour gaming event, and several social gatherings that last two or three hours each.

And here is how we do it.

> The Molaskey Group actively promotes events at The Pub. This includes: producing customized digital art posters for our sponsors; placing Second Life® event announcements and Second Life® classified ads; sending out Molaskey's Pub group notices; doing Web site promotion at MolaskeysPub.com; and providing on-site event hosts.

Code of Conduct

In your business plan, you may want to establish rules for employee conduct in-world when they are representing your company. Most businesses will have a Code of Conduct for their employees to use as a guide for expected behavior while representing the company. Such a code usually includes a discussion of ethical, moral, and legal responsibilities. A code of conduct says essentially that, although you are in the virtual world where freedom of expression is encouraged, as long as you are representing your company for business, you are expected to maintain professional interaction at all times. The Molaskey Group has the following mandate in our business plan:

The staff of The Pub make an effort to be friendly and helpful to people
of all virtual-world abilities and experience.

Professionals who wish to have an off-the-time-clock virtual life often have an avatar
for business and another for recreation, keeping the business version separate from
their less inhibited side.

2. The Market

The virtual-world market is still widely misunderstood. The people who are regularly
using Second Life® have the rest of the real world wondering what the big deal is and
what is so revolutionary about it. The answer is the ability to interact through communication in real time. Second Life® will not replace your traditional Web site or
other means of communication, but it will work with them. Second Life® can work
as an accessory to your Web site, offering customers a new online experience and
real-time interaction with your products and with customer service specialists. You
have the opportunity to interact with your customer base nearly face to face. The
marketing-related question you need to ask yourself is how do you make that work
for you? How you take advantage of that immense potential is entirely up to you.

Most companies want a fast return on investment (ROI) and are therefore concerned with the number of people encountering their product advertisements. If marketing efforts lead to someone viewing an advertisement, that is equal to what is called
an impression. The more impressions that occur, the greater the percentage of sales
will be. But in Second Life®, modern marketing professionals have to consider the
quality of their customer's experience with their brand. Some real-world, name brand
companies have fallen on their faces in Second Life® because they did not heed the advice of seasoned virtual-world professionals and forged ahead using traditional marketing plans in a vastly different market.

Brand name alone will not be enough to stand on in the virtual world. In
Second Life®, visitors will come if you build a worthwhile destination that is staffed

and content-fresh. Let everyone know who you are, what you do, and where to find you. This can all be done affordably but will require continuous maintenance. Both big and shoestring budgets can maintain a successful Second Life® site, as long as they keep their expectations of the virtual-world market realistic.

A business plan therefore requires you to think about and discuss your market before entering it. You will discuss your customers, market size and trends, competition, and estimated sales. In Second Life®, the market is "The Virtual World." Evolving from the World Wide Web, the virtual-world market is a global Internet marketplace with interactive 3D qualities.

Customers

When people visit a Web site, it is usually for a few minutes and a few pages. When people visit a virtual-world site, like Molaskey's Pub, it is for an hour or two or more, depending on the events and activities we offer. Without doubt, the virtual world offers a new breed of consumer: the interactive consumer. Virtual-world customers are diverse in every way. They are from every background, education level, skill level, and personality—and from countries around the world.

Because of the immense diversity of interactive customers, your business plan must identify your target segment. Are your customers from a specific country? Do they speak a certain language? Are they representing other Second Life® businesses? Or are they people who are in-world for recreation? Are they interested in education, music, the arts, or sports? It may be better to identify them by their interests, because people in Second Life® are often exploring lifestyles and identities that are unavailable to them in the real world. So describe them as avatars, respecting online choices that may be very different from the ones they would make in the real world.

Market Size and Trends

In this section of the business plan, it is important to describe the markets in all worlds—in-world, real world, and mixed reality, when both the real world and virtual world are used simultaneously. Although Linden Lab® does not disclose specific demographics of its residents, such as age, median income, etc., they do provide updated statistics such as the women/men ratio, transactions generated in L$, countries using Second Life®, and resident time online.

Competition

Businesses entering Second Life® may find competition lively, but not fierce. This social network is still in its formative years, where growth and development are occurring rapidly.

For this section of your business plan, cruise around in-world and do thorough research. You need to know what you're up against in terms of products and services, advertising, and pricing. The most competitive fields include developers, designers, and scripters—the people actually building the user-created world of Second Life®. General products and services are still experiencing friendly competition.

Estimated Sales

Your sales estimates depend on the products and services your business will provide. The best way to project sales is by doing market research.

A Second Life® business in development can expect the first three months to be a trial-and-education period, with a slow start to sales. Once you get the swing of how things work in-world, sales will noticeably improve and steadily increase as the population increases and your in-world skills improve.

Some businesses have stated they are making about U.S.$15,000 a month or more, whereas others have only made about U.S.$30–300. Many of the more successful companies attribute their high income to strategy and dedication to their virtual-world businesses.

An average musician with a following can make about L$50,000 a week for several performances or approximately $185. Using L$200,000 divided by 270 (the average rate of conversion to U.S. dollars), that's about U.S.$740 a month for a few hours a day, five days a week. Most musicians don't perform in SL™ that much, but the potential is there for comparison.

According to Simone Stern, a successful digital haute couture shop owner, sales ebb and flow as they do in real life. As you project sales, keep in mind that seasons change, holidays come and go, and trends explode and then die out.

3. Pricing and Sales Strategy

Discuss your pricing strategy in your business plan. As in the real world, supply and demand dictate the market rate; that is, the right price is what people are willing to pay for a product or service. Important questions to ask when setting your price point include:

- What does it cost you to produce a product or service?
- What percentage do you expect to make in profit?

The in-world currency, the Linden™, exchanges at approximately L$270 to each U.S.$1. This can be confusing when trying to establish a fair market rate for your product and services (L$10,000 = U.S.$37.03, approximately based on 10,000/270). So you may earn L$50,000 for a job and in real dollars earn $185. You need to determine what you're willing to trade for your (real) time and skills on the virtual-world market. For services, such as business development, promotion, and the like, the fair market rate remains what it is in the real world. Professionals in Second Life® do not decrease their rate for the virtual world. In fact, skilled professionals like graphic artists and designers may find an increase in their value as a result of their virtual-world skills.

4. Virtual World Development and Production

Consider the time it will take for your 3D builders to completely develop your plans as desired. When you find a capable builder, one who has demonstrated the ability to work well with you and has innovative ideas to develop your virtual world business, hire them. Payment arrangements must be clearly established, usually coinciding with the production and timeline of the project. The more interruptions they have, the slower the production. Have a discussion with them at the onset of the job and make sure they have the necessary permissions to build on your land and the materials they need, then let them work. As you see the building taking form, offer your concerns and praise.

If you have a large project, consider opening up in phases. Start with your reception area, or landing spot. Then place a sign indicating the anticipated grand opening and links to your website in the interim.

Many skilled builders will have site building down to a science, however, each new build is a custom-made masterpiece. You could have a fully constructed site in as little as a day or week, but the more exceptionally detailed builds will take a month or more, depending on the size and details of the project. Make sure you understand the timeline your builder is on.

5. Advertising and Public Relations

In this part of your business plan, communicate just how you will reach your target market. Detail the avenues that you will pursue on a regular basis, as part of a product launch, or in some other special promotion. Advertising and promotion in Second Life® is easy and inexpensive. Once you have a logo, form a group, display a billboard, and create a mission statement about your product or service, you can then easily reach customers using the following avenues:

- An in-world classified advertising system, searchable only in Second Life®

- Multiple Web sites, dedicated to promoting Second Life® products and services, including the SLExchange and OnRez, as well as within Ebay and other online shopping sites

- Your own Web site, perhaps the best of all means of promotion

You can also get creative with your promotion. Companies give away free t-shirts for avatars with their logos or products on them. Consider sponsoring events to get your product promoted along with the main attraction or to drive traffic to your establishment. Events can include private concerts, new product demos, game competitions, lectures, and guest appearances. Then be sure to create an Internet blog about your Second Life® events. That way, avatars who weren't there will find out just how much they're missing and be sure to be there next time.

Like real life, there is nothing like word of mouth. Creating buzz in Second Life® depends on the quality of your product, service, or destination. Unless you launch a calculated campaign, you can't count on this as a means of promotion, but if you deliver on your promises, customers will notice.

6. Business Management

An essential part of your business plan will include a discussion on how you will manage your business. The Small Business Association recommends that your plan address the following questions:

- How does your background and/or business experience help you in this business?

- What are your weaknesses, and how can you compensate for them?

- Who will be on the management team?

- What are their strengths, weaknesses, and backgrounds?

- What are their duties?

- Are these duties clearly defined?

- What are your current personnel needs?

- What are your plans for hiring and training personnel?

- What salaries or rates will you offer?

Maintaining an On-Site Presence

Although you may work on an eight-to-five work schedule, the virtual world runs 24/7. It is possible to set up a sales vending system and suggest that people contact you by e-mail for assistance when you are offline. However, serious business builders (those making a considerable investment and looking for ROI) should consider staffing their site with specially trained avatars. If you are a global brand, consider keeping your virtual-world doors open and staffed around the clock. You may find it is well worth paying a part-time avatar to manage the site during your off-hours.

The most successful businesses in Second Life® offer great customer service. They have someone on site to answer questions, demonstrate products, troubleshoot technical problems, and socialize with the customers.

Consider a real-world analogy. A well-known store opens up in your neighborhood. When you visit, the doors are open and the lights are on, but no one is there to welcome you and assist you. So you go through the store and ask, "What's the point?" Then you leave. That's a trap you don't want to fall into in the virtual world. Your virtual store is not a Web site; it is meant to be interactive. Anticipate your peak hours of business and staff accordingly.

Even if you schedule people to be there when you're not, they shouldn't just stand there and wait for people to come. Consider having them host special events. Because this is a global marketplace, these special events can be scheduled to accommodate any time zone. The point is to keep it fresh and interesting.

7. Financial and Legal Considerations

Financial Considerations

If you're out to make money in your Second Life® business, you will need to plan for your expenses and balance them with your projected income. This is one of the best ways to ensure that your business will remain open and profitable. Even if your livelihood does not depend on this income, you will want to maximize opportunity by managing costs. You don't want to be dipping into funds that you depend on if business in the virtual world takes a turn for the worse. Even in Second Life®, many potentially successful businesses fail because of poor financial management. As a business owner, you will need to plan so that you can meet your financial obligations and make a healthy profit along the way.

The best way to plan a budget is to determine the amount of money that you need to get started with and the amount needed to stay open. This is the baseline from which you will operate.

Start-Up Expenses

The expenses and capital requirements for a start-up in Second Life® are small compared to those of real-life businesses. Some of the most successful entrepreneurial establishments have grown from minimal seed money, if any at all. Your computer, a high-speed Internet provider, and accessories such as headset and upgrades may be the biggest real-life expenses needed. In-world, your biggest expenses may be outfitting your avatar with skin and clothing, then building and decorating your business's real estate.

Corporations often want to enter Second Life® with a bang to maximize visibility and branding. They might want to contract Second Life® specialists for branding, building, and marketing their debut. These professionals could cost tens of thousands of dollars, but the money will be well spent.

In your business plan, be sure to cover the following start-up expenses:

- Premium membership if you plan to own land

- Legal and professional fees, an LLC, etc.

- Equipment such as computers and upgrades

- Insurance (large companies consider this)

- Advertising and promotions

- Salaries/wages

- Accounting costs

- Income

Even though you may not be open for business, prepare an operating budget so that you can base your projections on reality. When you prepare this budget, make spending decisions according to the priorities you communicated in the business's description. To be safely in the black until you get the word out about your product or service, your operating budget should include enough money to cover the first three to six months after you open.

Your operating budget should allow for the following expenses:

Operating Budget

- Premium membership if you own land

- Advertising and promotions

- Legal and accounting

- Miscellaneous expenses

- Insurance

- Supplies

- Salaries and wages

- Income through dues, subscriptions, fees, and sales

- Taxes

Legal Considerations

Even though this is a virtual world, real-world laws apply. In Second Life®, it is still illegal to use copyrighted material without permission from the owner.

Intellectual Property Rights

The Digital Millennium Copyright Act (DMCA) is a United States copyright law that implements two 1996 WIPO treaties. It criminalizes the production and dissemination of technology, devices, or services used to circumvent measures that control access to copyrighted works (commonly known as DRM) and the act of circumventing an access control, even when there is no infringement of copyright itself. It also heightens the penalties for copyright infringement on the Internet. Passed on October 12, 1998, by a unanimous vote in the United States Senate and signed into law by President Bill Clinton on October 28, 1998, the DMCA amended title 17 of the U.S. Code to extend the reach of copyright, while limiting the liability of online providers from copyright infringement by their users.

8. Exit Strategy

During the planning stages of your business plan, you need to consider your exit strategy as well. The most responsible plans include a way in and a way out. This is not just for emergency planning; it is for the best of situations too. An exit plan means you won't just disappear or make any abrupt moves without letting those involved with your business understand what you are doing. It's a courtesy and a necessity when dealing with intellectual property.

Perhaps you are on to something very popular. Another company might make you an offer, and an exit plan includes the conditions in which you would accept a buyout. Include the minimum buyout figure you would use as a baseline to begin negotiating. In outlining your strategy, consider other terms that you would want to negotiate. For example, you may want the new owner to carry on your legacy and need to be committed to the mission that you established.

Ways to Use Your Business Plan

Now that you've done all this thinking, planning, and strategizing, you might be tempted to throw the document in a drawer and forget about it. Bad idea! What you have created is a useful guide to starting and running your business. Refer to it frequently. Because it is a living document, alter it to reflect changes in the market and how you conduct business. Second Life® is a lively and dynamic environment, and you want to grow with it.

- Give your mission statement to employees or people who inquire.

- Use portions of the business plan to develop marketing materials.

- Compare the financials: Are you where you thought you would be?

- If things are tight, can you cut expenses in a way that doesn't interfere with quality and service?

These are just a few examples of how your Second Life® business plan will help you far into the future.

6.

Netiquette and
Codes of Conduct

Some of the biggest attractions of Second Life® are the freedoms associated with individuality and society. People enjoy the freedom of expression, the freedom of creativity, the freedom of activity, and the freedom of association. Second Life® is an art. It is a living, interactive work of social art for which technology is the medium. People from around the world with every possible background and culture participate in Second Life®. People independently find one another, forming groups and societies in which to interrelate. Though many Second Life® communities like to portray themselves as offering a fulfilling, open-minded, and free society, the challenge has been in determining what that means.

The Internet was and continues to be criticized for crime, pornography, and other misuses. Just as crime seeps into everyday life, the online world is certainly no exception. In fact, for malintending people, it has been an opportunity. In the early days, the Internet's environment could be called dirty. Identity theft and piracy became rampant, and misinformation and spam circulated quickly, raising many questions about security, both personal and global. Over time, to gain credibility and popular appeal, the Internet had to polish a tarnished image. Laws were established to include the Internet and intellectual property rights and to protect the global economy, as well as personal and intellectual property. Copyright laws now include online distribution. In addition, the public has become wised-up to online antics. Spam is largely ignored and considered a nuisance to be deleted. Though these laws and practices are challenged every day, they have addressed major concerns on the use and development of the Internet.

Gaming

Many people are finding their way to Second Life® for gaming. Sim owners buy game tables as a way of attracting traffic to their land while getting a percentage of the prize money. It's an easy way to provide entertainment and produce an income. The gaming community represents a large majority of Second Life® residents.

The rules for gaming and gambling in Second Life® were once unstructured. In this user-created society, residents were building, playing, and selling games for a hearty profit. Gambling was widespread. Until 2007, Second Life® casinos were among the most successful business opportunities available. Then, as Second Life® grew in popularity, big questions were raised about money trading hands, taxes, and the legalities of virtual world operations. The laws of California, where Linden Lab is based, states that online gambling is illegal, threatening to end all operations. When approached by the federal government, Linden Lab immediately complied and prohibited all gambling activities in Second Life®. The shutdown became known as The Gambling Bust of '07.

This was a shock to the gaming businesses. Many casinos just shut down and left. Aargyle Zymurgy decided to investigate the legalities further. Aargyle is a talented and successful Second Life® game maker. When the abrupt gambling ban took place in Second Life® in 2007, he immediately jumped into action as a community leader and questioned the ban. Because the Second Life® gaming ban included all gaming where money is exchanged, it was going to affect the economy and the community.

Aargyle states. "I've not gone to school for law, but I've studied a lot, had my name on a handful of patents (wrote some primary white papers), and handled a few court cases pro se." He proved that there is a vital difference in the legalities between monetary reward for "games of chance" and "games of skill." Aargyle's games are "games of skill" and therefore in compliance. "The games where a player does not influence the outcome of the game are banned. We design the games where it's about skill, not luck, and we've done empirical tests to demonstrate that." The only challenge was in getting the Second Life® governance team to understand that his games were not money-hungry slot machines.

Because of Aargyle's swift action and clear proof that there is a distinctive difference between games of skill and games of chance, hundreds of people saved their businesses by simply complying with the "games of skill" rule. It saved the gaming community from a total dismantling, which would have seriously affected the Second Life® economy and large gaming community.

Mature and PG Sims

The Sim Rating System

Linden Lab created Second Life® sims with a rating system:

- Mature sims

- PG-rated sims

- Teen Grid

Mature Sims

There are mature sims, where verified adults conduct themselves in a liberated manner if they so wish. Strong language, nudity, and acts of lewdness are permissible— or not, as determined by governing landowners. Being on a mature sim does not mean every day is a peepshow. Mature sims are not all run by hedonist landowners or risqué activity directors. "Mature" simply means total freedom to choose the conduct and the content of what is on your land. Molaskey's Pub is on a mature sim, and so there is no question about displaying virtual booze. By the way, we don't serve drinks at Molaskey's Pub. The Pub is a "help yourself" kind of open, conceptual bar. Whatever anyone is actually drinking while logged in to Second Life® and visiting Molaskey's Pub is out of our control. Though we are on a mature sim, we do not tolerate lewd, offensive, or hostile behavior. We are able to maintain a clean, mature establishment by simply setting a good example. The very *idea* of having a bar on any land other than a mature sim may be considered irresponsible.

PG-Rated Sims

When you are in a PG-rated sim, language and behavior should be consistent with that of a PG-rated movie or broadcast television. Many of the sims in the PG-rated areas are well-known, real-life companies and universities because their conduct is already compliant with the terms of a PG-rated sim.

Teen Grid

The Teen Grid is entirely separate from the main world of Second Life®. Teen Grid is strictly for those between the ages 13 and 17. The only adults in Teen Grid are the ones granted limited accessibility from Linden Lab. They include educators, mentors, and trained monitors. The teens get to enjoy Second Life® with their peers. They can play games, be silly, create 3D objects, buy, sell, network, and attend classes in Second Life®. There is no mature area of the Teen Grid. When teen residents reach their 18th birthday, they graduate to the main grid.

Self-Censorship

Although Second Life® residents are at least 18 years of age or older and considered mature, having areas designated for various kinds of content and behavior makes it easier to find your comfort zone. Although the Second Life® terms of service state what is expected of residents and their behavior, the communities definitively distinguish proper conduct. Keeping the risqué lifestyle separate from the business world in Second Life® is possible. It's done by proper zoning and by displaying Codes of Conduct of expected behavior. When residents know what to expect in the many areas of Second Life®, it makes it easier to have a free, though somewhat regulated, society.

Incidents of Indecency

The Internet is a powerful tool, available to all, and so is Second Life®. Anyone with a well-functioning computer and high-speed Internet connection can access what they want online. Although Philip Rosedale stated that they trace Internet protocol (IP) addresses as needed, banning and reporting certain users (given a reason to do so), you cannot initially filter out the good from the bad residents, including ingrates, to intellectuals and everyone in between. Yet people try to capitalize on the virtual world any way they know how. People using their online identity to carry out a hedonistic lifestyle, for example, are welcome to do so, as long as it doesn't impede on the rights of others or break any laws. Linden Lab conforms to all local, state, U.S. federal, and international laws, and it has taken measures to weed out criminal and inappropriate practices in Second Life®. Mostly, though, it is left up to the community to identify wrongdoings and to protect itself.

The Community Protects Itself and Its Reputation

The thriving communities of Second Life® are made up of thousands of people from every area of business, with every level of education, various cultures, languages, interests, personal goals, and skills and personalities. These self-formed communities find a common interest and work toward a common goal despite their differences.

Self-Censorship

There doesn't have to be a criminal incident for a community to act on its beliefs. One of the most popular events held each summer in Second Life® is Burning Life, the virtual world version of the real-life event, Burning Man (the annual art extravaganza in Block Rock City, Nevada). Linden Lab proudly manages the virtual-world event, assigning roles to outstanding residents. Apple MacKay (Jay Mahar) was asked to participate on the Interactive Architects team of Burning Life 2007. Selected artists are given strict criteria by which to exhibit their virtual-world sculpture, interactive art, and fun and exceptional creations of every kind. Team leaders see to it that all exhibits conform to the standards of this high-profile event and report to the event leader. The Burning Life 2007 event leader had a few disagreements about certain exhibits leading up to the opening day of the event. One exhibit was a colossal virtual bronze sculpture called Water is Life by Cheen Pitney, depicting a woman standing nude under a stream of running water, which pooled at her feet. The sculpture was a beautiful work of art, which made a statement about mankind's excessive use (and waste) of water. The event leader, a fellow resident, saw the sculpture and placed censor blocks over the private parts of the sculpture because, as he pointed out, it was in a PG-rated sim.

This act of censorship caused an immediate community uprising. Dozens of avatars surrounded the sculpture, stripped naked, and covered themselves with censor blocks in protest. The argument between artists and event leaders went on for hours. After receiving so much attention from the community and several reporters, the sculpture was moved to a mature sim, sans censor blocks.

They feel very strongly about what they're doing in Second Life®, and they're willing to defend, protect, and nurture the efforts of one another.

Once a community is established and functioning, the contributing members have an interest in building it up and protecting its physical condition and social reputation. As Dr. Colin Parris (Vice President, Digital Convergence IBM Research) points out, "the Internet = data, virtual worlds = people," and he goes on to explain that wherever there may be wrongdoing within strong communities, such as Second Life®, "the community protects itself."

In many high-traffic areas, when an incident occurs, there is a person onsite to speak with. If you cannot locate someone, you can usually contact managers and owners through message boards as needed. This is usually reserved to ask questions and make comments, but on occasion it is necessary to report incidents.

Griefers

An incident may be a technical glitch or inappropriate behavior by a so-called griefer, an avatar who causes intentional disruptions, like a protestor and troublemaker. Griefers are distracting and nuisances more than anything else. Even though an avatar can't be harmed, usually you can find the names of griefers and ban them from your land. In addition, they can be reported to Linden Lab. Linden Lab reviews incidents and decides on punishment. Punishment could be a warning or an outright ban from Second Life®, depending on the severity of the incident.

On occasion, at our Pub we have had a few griefers. Some wise guy came around and bombarded us with hundreds of indecent pictures that fell from the sky like a heavy rainstorm. It was a big distraction more than anything. We got his name and reported him. Apparently, because that was not his first offense, he was banned from Second Life®.

People are passionate about what they do in Second Life®, and they are willing to defend it and nurture it. The community as a whole has an interest in maintaining the Second Life® image as well as its healthy commerce.

Netiquette

Though standing up for something you feel strongly about is virtuous, it can also be done with diplomacy. The way you handle yourself in Second Life® is a good indicator of how you handle yourself in real life. Your manners and social skills play an important part of your personal experiences and business success in the social world of Second Life®.

If etiquette authority Judith Martin (no relation), also known as Miss Manners, were to explore Second Life®, perhaps she would be fascinated to learn how manners and social behaviors carry over in the virtual world.

There is a time and a place for everything. Most of the social cues important in the real world apply in the virtual world. Though there are no governments or rulers other than what the residents create themselves, this is not a hedonistic society. It is a global community. There are still behaviors that are appropriate and inappropriate in every situation.

Here are some rules of etiquette to follow:

- Keep a comfortable space between yourself and others.

- Staring is impolite.

- USING CAPS WHEN SPEAKING is equivalent to speaking loudly or even yelling. This may turn others off when they are speaking with you.

- Speaking out of turn or out of context is disruptive.

- Sitting around naked is acceptable only outside the PG sims, public events, business meetings, and similar areas. Avatars have the bodies of gods, we know, but don't think it makes people think better of you.

- Bling (flashy jewelry), scripted body parts (ahem), and other avatar accessories are lag makers. Don't go to big events wearing them. The number of people in the sim is lag enough.

- If you say you're going to be somewhere at a certain time, by all means, be there. If logging on to SL is not possible (this can be the case from time to time), use e-mail, phones, text messaging, smoke signals, Morse code. Just make sure you advise the person waiting for you.

- Don't randomly offer friendship to people you just met. People like to get to know one another or have a need to contact you before they add you to their coveted friends list.

- Overly aggressive friend seekers are eventually put in their place if they cannot take a polite hint to back off!

- Spamming groups with silly chat or advertisements are frowned upon (actually, you will be humiliated and ejected from the group). Group notices and group chat are reserved for owners and managers to notify the group of relevant events and news. It is not for members to strike up small talk with 500 people at a time.

- Pushy sales tactics are tacky.

- One good turn deserves another. If someone has done something for you, show your appreciation by doing something in return.

- Accept people for how they present themselves. Everyone deserves your respect until you have reason not to extend it.

Code of Conduct

As big businesses entered Second Life®, they introduced a wild frontier of online living to their employees. Employees of various companies were found participating in risqué activities while wearing their company group tag. That's a big no-no. Even off the clock, if someone knows you work for Company A, and they work for Company Z, a competitor, confidential information must not be casually offered, nor must the company's reputation be damaged by unscrupulous actions. Professionals who wish to have an off-the-time-clock virtual life often have an avatar for business and another for recreation, keeping the latter separate from their less inhibited side.

IBM was one of the first establishments in Second Life® to implement Netiquette, a code of conduct for employees in the virtual world. Princeton University and several other respectable establishments have a Second Life® Code of Conduct, which is successfully maintained.

When IBM announced Netiquette, an amendment to their company code of conduct created for the virtual world, it was received as a huge endorsement for virtual worlds. It says that, as employees are busy mapping out the Metaverse, they must adhere to their real-world Code of Conduct whenever they are conducting business in the virtual world. By establishing this, IBM is saying that Second Life® is a place for real business amid the social aspect of the virtual world. It is creating standards for its employees working in the virtual world, which carry over from traditional business practices despite the social atmosphere they were entering.

Make Your Mark Through Your Manners

If you do not conduct yourself in a professional manner or if you exhibit bad manners, business and social networking opportunities will come and go. It is vitally important to your personal and professional success that you take the virtual world seriously when it comes to your conduct and interactions. Remember that there is a real-world person behind every avatar, and that person could be either a passing ship in the night or an important connection proving to be a career booster.

Organizations in Second Life® have certainly made their presence known, but how do individuals with something to contribute to society make themselves known? Thousands of people using Second Life® have something to offer. Getting recognized for your talents and skills may not be so hard to do when you conduct yourself in a friendly and professional manner.

Individuals stand out in their groups for demonstrating leadership talents, professionalism, and social skills. No matter your real-world job title, you can take on a role that you are comfortable with. Perhaps by playing an active role with a Second Life® community, you will be recognized for it, and opportunities will arise.

Spirit of Collaboration

Many cogs are at work as the wheel of productivity turns. Sometimes, you are not sure you know how to carry out a big idea until you meet the people with the talents you need. People with skills stand out. We see many big projects in Second Life® taking form by people talking informally, then turning talk into something tangible. People in casual conversation come up with an idea about how to do something or make something better, and then enthusiasm gets a project in motion. People say they can do certain tasks, that they have the skills essential to the plan, or that they know someone who does. Before you know it, you have assembled a team of collaborators with an understanding of the project and the unique skills to carry it out.

Second Life® is a user-generated world that is constantly being improved by the residents themselves. We see it happening over and over again. People come to Second Life® to see what it's all about. They create their avatar, go to meetings, concerts, and parties, and they generally just make themselves part of the scene. Then, after they get their bearings, they start to see how a user-generated world really works. There are plenty of great ideas to be realized and put into production by the talented people willing to act on them.

But these collaborators wouldn't last long on a project if it weren't for the unspoken rules of conduct and netiquette. Communication and trust would break down, a great project could be abandoned, and all that potential business would be lost. Following social cues are an important part of business success, and the virtual world is no exception.

All for One, One for All

The communities formed in Second Life® are so strong because they inherently work together to bring each other up. That is, out of nowhere they were created in a virtual world. Second Life® communities are formed with purpose, dedication, and a belief that what they are doing is important.

Many organizations do serious business in Second Life®; so when they are in-world representing their company or association, no one has to tell them the codes of conduct. They are not there for the wild side of Second Life®. Although real-life companies coming in to Second Life® are establishing formal rules of conduct for their employees, the communities and groups already established in Second Life® undoubtedly understand the rules. They were the ones who wrote them.

VIRTUAL-
WORLD
BUSINESS
VALUES

7.
Commerce

Though the social use of Second Life® is the most often celebrated, the emerging virtual-world marketplace and new industries forming have people contemplating strategies and new possibilities. Every day, $1.5 million trade hands in Second Life®. That's not accounting for the invoicing between two parties for Second Life® services. There are so many possibilities for new businesses to explore Second Life®—in marketing, entertainment, networking, branding, and education—that it can be as overwhelming as it is exciting. Dr. Colin Parris recognizes the "core business values" Second Life® has to offer, and he places these core business values in three categories:

1. Commerce

2. Education

3. Coordination and Innovation

We discuss commerce in this chapter, education in Chapter 8, and coordination and innovation in Chapter 9.

Doing Business in Second Life®

When the Internet provided a platform for a global marketplace, it changed not only the reach of business, but also how consumers responded to a brand they found on-line. Creating a Web site in tune with a company's product, service, and vision became a business necessity. The Web site makes an impression on potential customers, employees, and competitors, while providing pages of information and e-commerce at the point of sales. Mom-and-pop companies were competing in the global marketplace with large established companies hundreds of times their size. Commerce in Second Life® offers the same potential but in the third dimension, enabling customers to become immersed in your brand, interact with your products, and engage with helpful sales people in an entirely new and interesting way.

Once people get the hang of it, they pop in and out of Second Life® as easily as they do the Internet or use the telephone. Customers may spend a good hour at your site in Second Life®, testing your products, chatting with salespeople, and connecting with your brand. While they're spending quality time at your site, they're keeping away from your competitor. Second Life® is gradually changing the communication preferences of individuals and businesses around the world. Your virtual-world presence will become as important as your 800 number or Web site.

Virtual-world commerce is all about product and consumer experience, so it is important to focus on creating an engaging interactive environment. Here are some don'ts and do's.

Don't:

- Set up shop and leave it unattended. It is equivalent to opening up a shop on Main Street, putting out vending machines, and leaving with the door open for customers to just help themselves. It's very impersonal.

- Try to build your company site unless you're a skilled 3D builder. You wouldn't try to build your company Web site unless you had the specific skills to do so. A professional virtual-world site should, in fact, be done by a professional.

Do:

- Get involved with the Second Life® community by joining active, relevant groups and attending Second Life® classes and events.

- Form a group on behalf of your company so that you can be found through the Second Life® search engine.

- Hire a skilled, experienced 3D builder from Second Life® to build for you. Your building and its surroundings provide a lasting impression on your audience.

- Announce your company's presence in Second Life® with a press release.

- Personally invite real-world customers to visit your Second Life® site. Snapshots from Second Life® displaying your product or logo on your invitation will intrigue them.

- Have an experienced Second Life® resident on staff to welcome visitors. Everyone loves personal attention.

- Sponsor events to let the Second Life® community know you're there.

- Remember to have fun. If you're not enjoying your presence in Second Life®, neither will your customers.

Second Life® has the ability to significantly transform industry and society. It's just a matter of taking an established brand, event, or service from an impersonal 2D page on the Internet to an immersive, interactive 3D environment in Second Life®. You can import your current brand used on the Web and redesign it entirely in three dimensions, an easy way to create a brand environment and product utopia.

Product Immersion

Real-world brands and companies may use Second Life® to provide a virtual-world showroom, customer service center, and live event venue. You can establish a virtual-world site as an added value to your Internet Web site, making customer *experience* a top priority. When I see a company's Web site with a link to their location in Second Life®, I know that company is not only on the cutting edge of technology, but it has a vested interest in providing their customers with personalized attention, valuable information, and a positive experience with their products and services.

A motorcycle company, for example, may find having a virtual-world showroom a fun way to engage their customers. Motorcycle enthusiasts can build their own motorcycle in the virtual world using simulated real-world parts, such as engines, saddles, handlebars, different chrome and paint, and they can add the sound effects of an actual motorcycle. Then, the avatar-customer can take the custom-built masterpiece for a test ride. If your showroom is on your own island, you can offer them a ride through different terrain and atmosphere, such as an oceanside highway, a long stretch of asphalt through a desert, or a winding mountain road. Customers can then experiment with variations of their dream cycles, changing parts and accessories until they are undoubtedly satisfied with it. The potential in this idea is to have a virtual-world salesperson bring customers through the process of selecting and experiencing the product in the virtual world.

Making a major purchase such as a custom motorcycle or even a home appliance through Second Life® is still unheard of, though in years to come that may change. What is currently achieved through Second Life® is brand presence in an emerging market, new product introductions, sales presentations, and customer service. Second Life® is very effective for experiencing a brand or product, not just by seeing it, but by becoming part of the experience.

Customer Immersion

Customers who go to your Web site are able to see pictures, view imbedded video, read stories, get information, and click on links to other informative sites. Their visits average three minutes.

However, customers who go to your Second Life® site not only see pictures, but take pictures of themselves surrounded by your brand! Like a Web site, they can touch on screens to play video, read text, and click on links to Web sites. But the biggest difference is that they can walk around and engage with others while in your brand environment. It becomes a personal experience. They are immersed in your brand more so than in any Web site or television commercial. And they spend an average of 30 minutes to an hour at your site. That's more than ten times the visit length at your Web site.

Major motion picture companies have used Second Life®'s rich, 3D graphics for promoting film releases. Audiences not only get to learn about stories and characters, but they get to experience them first-hand by visiting a replica of the movie set created in 3D. They can try on costumes from the movies and play with the props. This is an entirely new way of engaging an audience. The virtual world provides an added business value to either the real world or the celluloid world, as the case may be.

Experience the Magic

The V3 Group (www.TheV3Group.com), established in 2006 by Odin Liam Wright, also known in Second Life® as Liam Kanno, introduced the movie industry to Second Life®. Liam's first client in 2006 was The Picture Production Company (www.thePPC.com/silverscreen), a film industry marketing agency. Creating an immersive world is nothing new to the film industry, but Liam showed them how to take it further using the 3D world of Second Life®.

The V3 Group created the Silverscreen Sim, where they promote virtual-world movie junkets for real-world movies such as *300*, *Transformers*, *Die Hard 4*, and *Iron Man*. This impressive build offers visitors an immersive experience while they view movie trailers, pick up free virtual props, and even schmooze with some of the movie producers. The V3 Group, created for the virtual world, found success in providing the real world with a virtual-world business value.

Real-World Products and Services

Using the developing virtual world to market your goods and services is still considered experimental. We can compare it to using the Internet because that's our closest reference. The Internet is a global marketplace, and so is Second Life®. The Internet offers information and communication, and so does Second Life®. The difference with Second Life®, however, lies in the ability to see the people around you, in avatar form, while interacting with them. Second Life® not only enhances the online experience, it is creating a new global community and pop culture.

Marketing

Marketing your product in Second Life® is not as hard as it sounds. Traditional methods of marketing fail in Second Life® unless they are tailored to fit Second Life®. The community is resistant to real-world sales pitches. Instead, marketers may find their best bet is to be part of the culture, supporting the events that residents attend. In other words, they are better off being passengers on the ride, not the drivers.

A liquor distributor approached Molaskey's Pub to market some of its products. The distributor asked us to install a scripted wall unit displaying bottles of their product. When people clicked on the wall unit, a series of questions popped up on the screen asking them to verify their real year of birth (virtual proofing). Then a prompt asked what they would like to drink from the bar. They were given a choice of about ten items. The inquirers would make a selection, which would be delivered to their inventory, complimenting their choice for those in the room to hear. From the inventory, the people would select the drink and "wear" it. The drink was programmed (by the designer/scripter) to be held in the hand of the avatar. Every minute or so, the avatar would take a sip. After several sips, the drink would disappear, leaving the avatar to make another selection.

For added fun with the crowd, the drink was programmed to enter text in the open chat, which read something like, "Time for another Tanqueray" or "That was a great pint of Guinness." The best part was that you could prompt a response from the crowd this way. They saw chat come up, someone would make a comment, and the conversation kept the crowd going. Also, those holding drinks from the scripted bar were able to toast cheers to each other with a rousing remark programmed by the scripted drink. This was great fun. Not only was the product in context with the market, it interacted with the audience. In return, the liquor distributor received market information about consumer choices and loyalty while participating in the community.

Branding

In much the same way that the liquor distributor marketed its brands at Molaskey's Pub, other brands can make an impression on the Second Life® market. Companies associated with pop culture and trends, like Coca-Cola, are participating in Second Life®. They generated excitement with a contest in Second Life® to stylize a virtual-world vending machine. Participants were encouraged to go beyond the constraints of the real world, creating one that is more suited for the virtual world. When Coca-Cola came into Second Life®, it made a public splash with their contest announcement and with a healthy handful of publicity. The Coca-Cola brand is seen throughout Second Life®, though not overbearingly. The company was cautious enough not to smother the virtual world with its brand, but it successfully involved the community to establish the classic Coca-Cola image and bubbly lifestyle as being a part of the growing virtual-world community.

Promoting

Social networks prove a good audience for promoting musicians, artists, and performers. Based on popularity and marketing, social network participants enjoy being on the edge of the live, interactive scene. Musicians play to several small audiences, providing personal attention. The audience feels connected to the musician, creating a devoted following. One of the ways musicians get and maintain a large following is by playing at several venues around Second Life®.

But Second Life® is only one avenue for modern musicians to promote themselves. Many musicians have produced albums and CDs while participating in other online networks, such as thesixtyone.com. The definitive difference with Second Life® promotions is that they are live performances that give people more to talk about. Several musicians are being discovered this way, because scouts and record producers regularly attend performances in Second Life®, noting how an audience responds to a performance.

Artists love Second Life® because it is a visual world. They can display their artwork in a 3D space at very little cost. There are art galleries all over Second Life®. Some of the art is simply for sale as virtual home or office décor, though many are beginning to earn a living using Second Life® to promote their real-world artwork.

For example, Jeffrey Lipsky, known in Second Life® as Filthy Fluno, is an artist from Massachusetts that is using Second Life® to promote his real-world artwork. In fact, Second Life® is his latest subject. Jeffrey captures the energy, people, and atmosphere from Second Life® in vivid, abstract, narrative pastel drawings. He is able to successfully market his work in the real world as well as in Second Life®, where he began an artist community. Jeffrey has been featured in *The New York Times Magazine*, among other publications, and blogs for his beautiful artwork and highly successful methods of bringing Second Life® into the real world through his art.

Networking

Social networking may seem to be the latest buzzword, but it is not a fad term. Social networking is the way in which we engage one another and build relationships. It has been done throughout history. We use our social skills to build connections in addition to our professional skills. In modern days, social networking happens at the speed of light, as the Internet has allowed. Instead of relying on attendees at trade shows and conferences to interrelate, where people are concerned with their looks, bad breath, number of business cards handed out and received, and other practical issues, people are networking relatively effortlessly and doing more of it online. There are several on-line social networks, each with a purpose. LinkedIn, for example, is a professional net-working site. Second Life® is a social networking site.

As communities are formed in Second Life®, it becomes easier to find a specific category of person to associate with. Like interests attract one another. I can't tell you how many times I have heard of people who casually mention things in conversation only for someone else to speak up and say they need or have what someone else is looking for. This kind of networking used to take months to unfold. Today, it happens in an instant.

Virtual-World Products and Services

Virtual-world products and services may be hard for the real world to understand because there is no tangible product, yet many thousands of people are making money this way. So how can it be so valuable? The answer has to do with supply and demand: See a need, fill a need.

Modeling the Real World

Members of the architectural and real estate fields are using Second Life® in creative ways to promote their real-world products.

Jon Brouchoud is an architect who came to Second Life® in June 2006. He saw Second Life® as a tool to help clients visualize design ideas for green residential projects from his real-life studio, Crescendo Design. Operating from a home studio in the Midwest United States, he began servicing real-world clients from a broad geographic region using Second Life®. He models design concepts from his office, and clients tour the designs in 3D from the comfort of their homes, for as long as they want. It's a great example of a virtual-world business value. From Keystone Bouchard's Crescendo Design Studio in Second Life®, you can purchase one of several stylish designs and blueprints to build a real-world Green Home. They're available for L$150,000 each, which is about $500.

Second Life® commerce spills into the real world in many ways. A property manager from Europe set up a quaint storefront in a Second Life® shopping district, putting up interactive posters of the real-life properties it features for rent around Europe. The posters included several pictures of the properties for rent, along with the property stats and rates. I was so intrigued by the beautiful, unique properties they featured that after spending more than an hour clicking through to all of the wonderful properties, I just about rented them on the spot and booked a flight to Portugal with my family!

Second Life® is a user-created world. What someone can't create, they buy, at an enjoyable exchange rate. People come up with really good ways of making money in a market like this. Quality virtual-world products and services are in demand. People freely spend L$300 to L$30,000 on virtual-world items everyday. That's about $1

to $111 per sale in real life, generating over a million dollars in sales in Second Life®
everyday.

Keeping inventory is not a problem. Once an item is created, you can make as
many copies as you need, for as long as you need. If you have the skill to create an item
someone else needs or admires, you can sell it, usually at a profit worth the time to
make it. (See Table 7–1.)

Table 7–1 Sample Products

Virtual Product	Professional	Approximate Rates
Buildings, landscapes, 3D content of any sort	Designer, builder, architect	$L5,000–L$150,000 or real-world all-inclusive package. Deals up to $50,000
Gadgetry, games, click-through signs, animations	Designer, scripter	L$300–L$5,000
Avatar refinement Skin, hair, clothes, costumes, and accessories	Fashion designer	Free—L$2,500 Free items given to newcomers as an incentive
Home, yard, holiday, and office decor	Shop owners	Free–L$1,500

Virtual-world professional service providers, such as builders and developers, work
out an agreement to be paid in real-world currency or Linden dollars with a 30-day
contract and 50% payable upon signing, depending on the scope of the job. Just because it is work in a virtual world, the terms of work and fees are as real as life itself.
Because these are real-world services on a virtual-world project, the fee dollars need
to be converted: L$50,000 is not the same as $50,000, but rather about $185.00. If a
builder provides you with a custom-built property, taking 5 to 10 days of part-time
hours to do it, don't think twice about paying it. This is standard practice in Second
Life® commerce. (See Table 7–2.)

Table 7–2　Sample Services

Situation	Service	Approximate Rates
Event management: venue rental, hosts, entertainment, promotional material	Event promoters	L$50,000–L$150,000. Also invoiced through real-world LLC
Event host/greeters	Event host/greeters	L$300–L$500 per hour
Entertainment	Musicians, comedians, actors	L$3,000–L$10,000 per hour
Promotional material	Advertising/photography/public relations	Negotiable
Finding places around Second Life®	Tour guide	L$200–L$400 per person
Portrait photography	Photographers	L$250–L$500 per session

Many services, such as photography, counseling, tour guiding, and party planning, are paid in Linden dollars at the time the service is rendered. On one side of the commerce in Second Life®, you are a service provider; on the other, you're the customer.

As the virtual world is developing, so are the needs of its users; therefore more opportunities to develop business will arise. People will continue to form new companies based on the refinement needs of the virtual world. If there is an idea or software to enhance user experience, technology gadgetry, or even fashion for the vanity of the avatars, there is plenty of opportunity to participate in the healthy commerce in the virtual world.

Combining Real-World Experience with In-World Needs

Real-world graphic artists and computer programmers are finding Second Life® an obvious market for their real-world skills. They can easily earn an income if they apply themselves, either part time or full time, because their skills are in high demand in the virtual world. What may not be obvious is how people with other skills can do the same.

You do not need to be a graphic artist to succeed in Second Life®. Plenty of other skills come in handy. There are people with very limited computer skills who succeed in Second Life® because of their social and organizational skills or management skills, for instance. Those skills are applied to running a virtual-world business or event as they do in real life.

At Molaskey's Pub, we are able to use our real-world professional skills to launch a unique brand from the virtual world into the real world. Kathey Fatica, known in Second Life® as Katydid Something, is our Molaskey's Pub partner, and she owns an ad agency in real life. When Molaskey's Pub needs billboards, posters, and banners, Kathey happily does them in her signature style from her office at Needham Fatica. She also has people skills, which come in handy in a busy pub in a social network. Kathey's real-world skills play an important role in Molaskey's Pub synergy and image.

Bringing Your Virtual-World Brand into the Real World

Hardly anything is more satisfying to an entrepreneur from Second Life® than to see your brand displayed, worn, and recognized in the real world. Because this has been happening for Molaskey's Pub, we proudly continue to nurture business and promote our brand, born in the virtual world.

Virtual-world brands are successfully reaching the real world. Molaskey's Pub began as an exercise in 3D building and social networking, and it has evolved into an iconic virtual-world brand now recognized in the real world.

Here's how Molaskey's Pub is doing it:

- First of all, we are fortunate to have the right mixture of real-world professionals who serendipitously met in Second Life® and who share a commitment to building and developing the Molaskey's Pub brand and experience. That includes owners, staff, musicians, and patrons.

Feeling Lost in Second Life®? Take a Tour!

Delphina Audina is a marketing manager from Austria with a masters in business administration and a broad background in tourism, interactive media, e-marketing, and strategy management. She has experience from the national tourism board promoting travel packages and was the commercial director for an interactive travel agency.

When she joined Second Life® in December 2006, Delphina searched for things to do and see. What she often came up with was a handful of outdated landmarks and misleading information. As she grew tired of wandering aimlessly around the vast virtual world, Delphina came up with the idea of providing a service of recommending worthwhile places and exciting events and giving tours around Second Life®. It was a great, sensible idea, so she acted on it. Matching her real-life tourism skills with an obvious need in Second Life®, she came up with a business plan for a Second Life® tour guide agency. Touring around Second Life® never gets boring. It would take a lifetime to see all there is to see. Going on a field trip with a field guide is fun, informative, and a great idea.

- Molaskey's Pub has mass appeal. It's The Global, Neighborhood Pub. The Pub is a professional-grade, visually pleasing structure that emulates a real-life quality pub found anywhere in the world. We have joked, as we sit around the virtual bar enjoying banter, that it feels like being on the set of the popular show *Cheers*, and we laugh and sing, "Molaskey's Pub, Where everybody knows your name because it's typewritten over your head."

- We go out of our way to make people feel at home. People enjoy being part of our establishment.

- We developed Molaskeys-Pub.com, where we post articles, pictures, video clips, and a schedule of events.

- We regularly host great events at Molaskey's Pub and notify our group with an invitation. Our live music concerts draw crowds three times a week. We also have games and parties, so traffic is consistently good. We established a strong virtual-world presence.

- We have friendly hosts that recruit new members while retaining long-standing members.

- We get several mentions in popular blogs and have even gained the attention of national reporters.

- We're active members in other relevant groups and communities, such as the education, business, artist, and musician communities.

- We attend real-world and virtual-world conferences and sponsor events using the Molaskey's Pub logo. We even had Molaskey's Pub business cards and embroidered shirts made. We have people in the real world asking, "Where IS Molaskey's Pub?" We're getting the word out there.

Molaskey's Pub was created as a networking and 3D building exercise. It developed into a popular destination recognized in the real and virtual worlds because we provide a quality product: our virtual-world venue. We have the right mix of people, a beautiful place, quality entertainment, and themed parties. We're involved with different communities, and we receive continuous publicity and support from the community we serve.

Innovation Is the Key

Businesses are using the 3D user-created immersive technology of Second Life in groundbreaking ways, and you are welcome to join. There is no one way of going about your business. It's a fluid market that benefits from your contribution. New businesses have been and will continue to be established to refine our experience of this user-created world.

8.
Education and Training

Education is considered a Second Life® core business value because it is an effective distance learning environment. You can gather many students from remote locations and provide instruction in a secure online 3D environment very affordably. Whether you need to teach 3, 30, or a 100 people at a time, education and training can be effectively and efficiently done using Second Life®. Learning institutions are also discovering how to use Second Life® effectively for group or personalized instruction. Businesses can establish team-based corporate role-playing for critique. Dr. Parris notes, "There is increased productivity when training in a virtual-world environment," and "it provides faster feedback at far lower cost."

Although distance learning can be done for business training and accredited courses, people need to be taught about the virtual world itself. The more employees and students know about social interaction and business dealings in the virtual world, the stronger your company or institution is. In the near future, virtual-world business training and university education will become an important part of modern business development. Distance education, human resource situations, and specialized training with companies and universities have just begun to see the potential in using Second Life®.

SL™-Persis Trilling and her team at the Princeton University Education Technologies Center, along with a crew of builders from Second Life®, made a virtual-world representation of the real-life Princeton University campus. I met with Persis to discuss how and why a university dating back to the eighteenth century is using the modern virtual world of Second Life®. As Persis states, "Leading indicators are that virtual worlds will be big in terms of social software within five years." Princeton University has an esteemed reputation of high standards and leadership. Its presence in Second Life® speaks volumes.

Of the nine islands owned by Princeton University: North, East, South, West, Forrestal, Groups, Alexander Beach, and Princeton University proper, four of those nine are planned for later use. The spectacular buildings and campus were built with a team of Second Life® builders and designers. It has been called the best example of real-world structures replicated in the virtual world. I can't argue with that. I have been to both the real-world Princeton University and the virtual one. The Princeton campus in Second Life® has some of the best work I have seen in all of Second Life®.

As one of the most notable universities in the world, Princeton established what it calls "exploration goals" when planning its presence in Second Life®. Since opening in 2007, the university uses its virtual-world campus for classes, research, and community outreach. As stated earlier, Princeton University does not offer distance education, but the Second Life® experience augments the face-to-face classroom experience.

Learning International Etiquette

Persis graciously demonstrated how a class at SL Princeton University is practicing international business etiquette in Second Life®. The members of the class created a program where you are in an international social and business scenario and have to decide the appropriate gestures for the culture in different situations. It is played out in real time through the avatar, giving clues to the student as part of the lesson. For instance, a participant from the Western World enters into a virtual-business situation in, say, the Middle East. A prompt describes the situation and offers choices on how to greet, compliment, or otherwise behave appropriately. The student chooses how to animate the avatar, whether it is to bow, shake hands, or hug, depending on the situation. The program also offers clues on appropriate dress and local cultures. Students practice these gestures and apply them to the real world.

A New Form of Art and Music

Princeton University supports several impressive 3D art installations and music events in Second Life®. Alexander Beach is home to an amazing conceptual design of modern architecture by Scope Cleaver, which the university uses for contemporary music, and Alexander Hall, which is representative of the real-world campus building, as the setting for a classical music concert.

Princeton University is also opening a new center opening that will create art that is "born digital." Persis recognizes, "There are some amazing artists in Second Life®." And these artists exhibit original digital artwork and astonishing immersive art installations.

When I visited the campus, DynaFleur was on exhibit in the Princeton South region. As I walked through the exhibit, my screen became filled with vibrant moving colors as if I were entering a live, futuristic flora the size of buildings. Douglas Story and Desdemona Enfield created a beautiful larger-than-life floral abstract. This was complemented by a special landscape created by Poid Mahovlich and a sound movement designed by Dizzy Banjo, remarkably created to respond to your presence as you walk through it.

PARSEC was another, highly intelligent, innovative, immersive virtual-world art installation on display at SL Princeton. PARSEC is an interactive "instrument" using seven avatars who control music and objects using only their voices. There is even a challenge to unlock a puzzle within the musical composition, using level voice tones. This is another one of Dizzy Banjo's compositions with Eshi Otawara as the creator of the PARSEC environment. The scripts are from Chase Marellan, a well-known programmer and author of many programming books, including the *Platform Second Life: Developing Real Life Applications* (Manning Press), coauthored with Jay Clarke.

The lesson learned from these exhibits and concert halls is to exercise your resources in new and creative ways, to explore and learn how to use the 3D interactive online platform. Extend yourself beyond the constraints of the real world by experimenting with physics and scale and depth perception as the virtual world allows. Give the world something to think about by creating totally innovative works. Some of the best visual and structural examples in architecture, art, music, international culture, and communication are found at Princeton University in Second Life®. Princeton's high standards evidently carry over into the virtual world.

Community Outreach: Alumni and Guests

The art at Princeton University is for display only. In fact, it doesn't sell anything. The shop items are posted at $0 to buy. I picked up a snazzy blazer for the occasional pomp and ceremony and a piece of heraldry to hang in the Pub. At the time of writing, all items were free. You can visit the SL Princeton store in the Forrestal region and pick up a fairly decent-looking ready-made avatar, Princeton banners, clothing, accessories, and a *New User Learning Tour HUD* absolutely free. Make sure you have time to tour the campus. It's a great place to explore.

One of the best-kept secrets Persis revealed during the campus tour is the availability to hear 15 years' worth of public lectures. They are free through University Channel off your iTunes, Podcasts, and Vodcasts. They will also be available through SL Princeton University.

The Princeton Groups region is the gathering spot for alumni, campus community, guests, research participants, student groups, organizations, environmental awareness groups, and the build group. On display are virtual trinkets, clothing, banners, and, for nostalgic alumni, even the iconic Princeton Tigers that guard Nassau Hall. The long, proud history of Princeton University is evident in this virtual-world extension of this famous institution. It is a tribute indeed.

When asked how she sees the virtual world shaping up in the next 5 to 10 years, Trilling commented on the virtual world becoming the way many people communicate, as important as e-mail and more immediate. In terms of creation, the virtual world is cheaper but not less challenging. Equipment, like cameras and building tools, are built into the program, so there's no need to buy them. But the skill required to produce and build are equivalent to those of the real world, and "those with the right skills are raising the bar."

Using the Virtual-World Classroom to Reach Generation I

The generation of people raised on the Internet and video games are naturally very comfortable in an online environment. Virtual-world classrooms offer the so-called Generation I an entirely new learning platform. This generation has exhibited a remarkable ability to learn and to apply complex strategies and maneuvers, as well as a few codes of conduct from playing video games. They're reading, competing, pre-planning, and demonstrating mathematical skills, all in the name of entertainment. But if you sit those students down in a crowded classroom and apply a standard curriculum that has been in place for 40 years, they quickly loose interest. Apply that lesson to the virtual world and see how these students show renewed interest in the lesson plan. I sincerely believe that people of all ages have an interest in learning. Sometimes the trick to teaching is to pique students' interest with a personalized method of learning.

As Generation I begin their careers in a corporate environment, making smart, split-second decisions, and working with others, their online skills and persona will come in handy. There is an obvious distinction between games and reality, but the strategies and thought processes learned from gaming are valuable exercises that can be used in the real world. The virtual-world method of teaching is being recognized and successfully practiced by some of the most respected institutions and companies around the world.

New Media Consortium

The New Media Consortium is a real-world, not-for-profit organization of 300 museums, universities, research facilities, and foundations from around the word, whose mission is to seek and use innovative technology collaboratively. They founded Second Life® several years ago and have been continually impressing its members with the numerous collaborative and educational possibilities that the virtual world presents.

The members of the NMC enjoy a full range of services, including development of their virtual-world presence and conferences and training for utilizing the virtual world to its fullest potential. Members of the NMC include California State University, Cornell University, Columbia University, Princeton, Harvard, Bucks County Community College, Rutgers, IBM Almaden Research Center, John Lennon Educational Tour Bus, and several hundred more. To date, not all institutions are involved with Second Life®, but, according to the NMC, over a thousand Second Life® islands were created in 2007 for educational and research facilities.

Several universities are conducting undergraduate classes in Second Life®. They convene online, exchange research findings, attend lectures, take tests, and ask questions. The online class offers added convenience because students and faculty can log on from their location of greatest convenience, whether it is from home, dorm, library, or office.

The NMC has introduced Second Life® to hundreds of institutions. Once these educators and researchers arrive in Second Life® and get their bearings, they are often inspired to set out on their own and form groups and communities.

Metanomics is an informational business group in Second Life® run by Robert Bloomfield of Cornell University, Johnson Graduate School of Management. Every week, the group meets to discuss different topics of business in the virtual world. During their gatherings, a guest speaker addresses the group, hosted by Bloomfield's avatar, Beyers Sellers. While the focus is on the guest speaker, the group makes commentaries and debates issues in the chat window. These are some of the most informative discussions on the development of virtual worlds I have ever attended.

As educational leaders are experimenting with the virtual world, learning how to create and confidently utilize a virtual classroom, we can credit the educational community for their interest and efforts in doing this.

Second Life® Education (**SLed®**)

Second Life® Education is an education community formed in-world. These K–20 educators are teaching one another how to use the virtual world of Second Life® as a valuable, cost-effective, exciting educational tool. They are learning about the virtual world, creating virtual classrooms, teaching others what they've learned, and preparing the next generation, as well as the current one, for the virtual-world classroom.

The SLed community offers ideas and examples of how and why people are using Second Life® for teaching. Education professionals in Second Life® convene regularly, exchange progress notes and concerns, offer solutions for problems (such as budget and experience), and discuss how using virtual worlds can enhance and improve current methods of teaching.

This is such a bold move for educators, but it is a necessary one, because there is tremendous potential in using virtual worlds for education. Teachers and librarians from all grade levels are planning lessons in Second Life®. They are proactively establishing virtual-world classrooms in preparation for the wave of interested students eager to learn about virtual worlds.

Practicing Real-Life Scenarios

Innov8, IBM's initiative to inspire Generation I through technology, has created a virtual-world environment with a game-like nature for the corporate environment.

David Lapp is the manager of IBM SOA and WebSphere Marketing (http://www-304.ibm.com/jct03001c/software/solutions/soa/innov8.html; http://www-306.ibm.com/software). Lapp explains Innov8: "This is the maturation of a generation raised on video games." These future business leaders understand the virtual-world environment for strategizing; now they are learning to use it to strengthen their real-world business skills.

Innov8 is a lesson designed for companies and business schools to effectively demonstrate real-time business decision making using virtual-world technology. For example, a professor goes to the IBM Web site, signs into the Innov8 program, and begins the lesson. Participants are guided through the game with a storyline, much like a video game, but this game takes place in a typical business office. Instead of leaping over lava pits and dodging arrows like Lara Croft, the participant is depicted as a business professional and given business-world challenges. Some of the challenges include a colleague casually strolling the hall on a personal call using his cell phone; while you try to get his attention to talk about business, he is oblivious to your timely needs. Game participants trot around the office finding specially located message boards while gaining valuable information for their time management mission. The ultimate goal is to identify the business process, strengths, and weaknesses, and then reinforce what works using technology.

IBM's Innov8 program is a learning tool with value that extends beyond the academia market in the business world; it's not just for business students. Business training for established professionals can also be performed this way. The tools can be set to modify the game with different scenarios. A program may be designed in the same manner for management or sales training. Virtual-world game playing is an efficient way to learn time management and real-time decision making.

The same tool may also be used for learning global business cultures. Effective communication across cultural borders is an important business skill that can be practiced in a program like this. You can create and program a private 3D environment for almost every need. Consult a 3D business developer with your goals, and see what innovative ways you can use to train employees.

In the emerging area of 3D interactive learning tools, you can expect to see "more and more of these applications."

Human Resource Training

The virtual world can be used to conduct human resource (HR) workshops, as well as for management training and demonstrations. Companies are finding this environment an interesting and cost-effective alternative to traditional classroom gatherings and video presentations.

At the Virtual World Conference in New York, we were given a demonstration of human resources at work in the virtual world. A virtual-world program presented different situations to avatars-in-training. They had to identify and discuss the situations and learn how to handle them appropriately. They were asked to identify inappropriate behavior in the workplace, such as sexual harassment or substance abuse. Unlike stale and dated videos with actors and a narrator, the program is a fun and interesting way of getting an important message out to employees. The immersive, real-time interaction is effective in getting the message across because attendees, not actors, participate in it.

HR directors can create private instruction programs and scenarios tailor-made to their training needs. Doing so requires the preplanning of courses and the building of an adequate virtual-world facility, but it is a low-maintenance structure, requiring a minimum of people to manage.

When you own a section of the virtual world, you can set your land to private and teleport workshop attendees directly to your meeting spot. Make sure you state your dress code requirements and provide attendees with your group tag, which works as a password, in order to get into the private area. Owners and designated officers of the group maintain the list of authorized members.

Virtual-world seminars can be a corporate world solution to gathering large numbers of people from all around the globe without breaking the budget. The classroom is maintained as a private area, so there are no distractions from the outside virtual world. Meetings can be as small as two people for private training or as large as 100 people at a time, depending on your sim capacity. Seminars can be done in phases, to accommodate a larger audience if necessary. These training seminars are attended from employees' homes or offices, and they receive a high rating of approval. There is likely no travel expense involved with having employees attend an HR or Town Hall meeting in the virtual world. Virtual-world training offers them the added value of convenience at lower cost, while accomplishing a great deal. And, of course, everyone gets a good seat and a chance to speak.

The interactive quality of Second Life® makes this option very practical. Companies are considering how to train their employees to use it for added efficiency and productivity. Employees enjoy it because it is intensely interesting and innovative. It makes them proud to be part of a company that adopts solutions that benefits everyone.

It is predicted that Second Life® educators are going to be among the most sought-after professions. Virtual classrooms are going to be filled with enthusiastic, attentive students from grade school to business school and everything in between.

Extending the Reach of Education

Not only are educators using Second Life® as a virtual classroom, researchers are studying the virtual world of Second Life®, how people use it, and how it can enhance their real lives. Those afflicted with social disorders, such as attention-deficit hyper-activity disorder (ADHD) and Asperger's syndrome, are finding virtual worlds a very liberating way of communicating and a possible avenue to an education and fulfilling profession. Adults with some degree of autism testify that communicating in a social network like Second Life® is much easier and enjoyable for them. For the millions of people whom autism directly affects, this certainly warrants further investigation. Simon Bignell, lecturer of psychology at the University of Derby, Derbyshire, United Kingdom (http://psychology.derby.ac.uk/~simon/staff/simon_bignell.html), received the support of his university to conduct research in Second Life® after demonstrating the uses of it for psychology skills, including his specialties: autism, ADHD, and Asperger's research.

Simon explained, as we toured the university campus in Second Life®:

> One experiment is looking at how virtual worlds can be used to benefit people with socio-communication problems. They are taking people with Asperger's syndrome into the lab and giving them different scenarios to try out. For example, one situation looks at whether text- or voice-based information is better. Another situation uses impoverished vs. rich communicative environments. It seems that people with high-functioning autism and Asperger's syndrome have problems keeping up with the flow of information in the exchange between verbal communicators. That is, that they report a preference for text-based communication because it has the advantage of forcing the information to be to the point.

Also, in Second Life®, there are all the advantages of virtual social interactions. When he is not conducting class, doing experiments, or lecturing, Simon makes himself available in Second Life® for intelligent discussions on the topic of autism and virtual worlds, but he says that he is not aiming to provide therapy this way. "My primary aim, though, is not to provide therapy or treatments, it's to seek knowledge about the utility of virtual worlds for people with these conditions. Then when we know much more we can start to think about how we might use them clinically."

Technology has played a part in helping people with autism. The virtual world holds the potential to generate a new market of skilled jobs unlike anything before. Autistics are intelligent, but they are generally isolated. Using the virtual-world platforms gives them the opportunity to socialize and strengthen professional skills in anonymity and comfort.

Because Simon was able to begin his research through the University of Derby, thousands of people afflicted with autism can follow his research through the years, perhaps finding suitable jobs through the comfort of a virtual-world platform.

Simon Bignell is known in Second Life® as Milton Broome. He also runs these SL groups: Autism Research, ADHD Research, Psychological Research, Virtual Psychology, University of Derby. He welcomes your comments and interest in his important research.

Free and Available Education

Second Life® thrives on its community. With so much to learn, community members have taken it upon themselves to mentor newcomers and even offer classes on improving the Second Life® experience.

There are several classes about and incentives to learn Second Life® basics. If you search "free classes" in-world, you will find at least a dozen places to go where someone will teach you the skills you need to advance your abilities in Second Life®.

You can learn the basics on how to make original content, such as clothing, jewelry, and structures, or you can learn how to animate or film machinima. All of these classes are offered to individuals free of charge, either through mentor programs or through the Second Life® Wiki.

A Change in Course, a Thirst for Knowledge

As we have demonstrated, the 3D simulator is being used as a learning tool by some of the heftiest hitters of the corporate and educational world. More and more businesses will take this path if they haven't already. Custom-created learning environments are going to be some of the most populated areas of the virtual world, servicing hundreds of people regularly. We see a great thirst for knowledge on virtual worlds happening on every level. Mitch Kapor has called Second Life® a "disruptive technology." In this relatively early stage of Second Life®'s development, Fortune 500 companies cannot yet fathom using this technology to replace their current methods of video conferencing, travel, and classrooms. But as they see how other reputable companies and universities are demonstrating the business value of virtual-world education and training, it will likely and eventually complement or even replace previous methods.

9.

Coordination and Innovation

Another virtual-world business value is coordination and innovation. As Dr. Parris explains, the virtual-world platform augments the Internet, providing an added dimension to online communication, allowing people to collaborate on projects and to exchange information and documents in real time despite where they are geographically. This core business value sums up the way in which people gather in the virtual world and use this technology for collaborative work, saving time and money. Virtual-world technology provides efficiency and synchronicity like never before.

Virtual worlds are certainly experiencing explosive popularity in the new millennium, but the user-created virtual world of Second Life® has a particular advantage over other virtual worlds through ownership, healthy commerce, and intellectual property. These are the main reasons why Second Life® is a valuable communication and business tool for individuals and companies. The two-dimensional Internet, video conferencing, or any other communicative ways of doing business are all still successfully used, but as the Metaverse develops in the hands of specialized 3D content creators and millions of virtual-world participants, you can expect a shift of interest to the virtual world for networking and conferencing. It's the most modern and innovative way for groups of people to collaboratively use the Internet.

Collaborative Communication

Aside from managing Molaskey's Pub, a social-based establishment, I belong to several business and educational groups in Second Life®, including Metanomics, The New Media Consortium, and The Non Profit Commons, to name a few. Every week, I make an effort to attend several regularly scheduled collaborations and lectures. I attend not because I am obligated to, but because I sincerely want to.

These gatherings give me great insight about people, community actions, and the tools that impact real and virtual life. I have attended a myriad of events and lectures, including the first cross-virtual-world discussion panel featuring There.com's CEO, Michael Wilson, who streamed live into Second Life®. I have also attended author readings, business discussions, lectures on the environment, and innovative virtual-world product demonstrations, refining the virtual-world experience. When I attend, it is mostly as an observer, multitasking in real life as I listen. I find myself in the company of highly educated professionals, talented virtual-world developers, and their entourages. Sometimes I participate in the discussion, offering my two cents. And sometimes my two cents count.

Just adding commentary or perspective to the group discussion can trigger a debate or an idea that contributes to the quality of the discussion. That's the beauty of collaborative communication in the virtual world; it's a melting pot. You have the opportunity to be in the presence of and participate in discussions with an eclectic gathering of professionals, entrepreneurs, artists, and educators. To schedule gatherings like these in real life would require an exorbitant amount of time, scheduling, travel, expense, and energy. In Second Life®, such gatherings of professionals and educators happen regularly, at no cost, without pomp and circumstance. Yet the same important message or interesting lecture is successfully carried out. These unique gatherings don't seem to be happening anywhere else but in Second Life®. Real-time commentary on rich topics from each of these valued perspectives really seasons the virtual stew.

These groups, which can now boast a thousand members or more, started out as an idea to gather people with like interests in Second Life®. They created missions and outreach through group communication and a lecture series with relevant topics of discussion. Group membership and participation increased, and more ideas were presented for members to explore and act upon. Group members became familiar with one another and often decided to work together on projects, for the group or independent of it.

The contacts made and networking achieved through these gatherings make up most of the relationship building and collaboration in Second Life®. I have attended many scheduled events at which a discussion leads to an idea and then two or more people take the lead and develop the idea into a collaborative project for either the virtual or real world. The next time the group gathers, they present their idea or discuss its progress. As a result, the collaborators often develop a professional relationship and even a friendship.

Not all collaborative work projects in Second Life® are performed by newly formed virtual relationships. One of the most useful ways real-world companies

Working Together to Build Our Cities

Having a 3D interactive virtual world in which to construct buildings and neighborhoods has its advantages for architects and city planners because of the creative and collaborative aspects the virtual world allows.

Architects are not the only ones having fun designing in Second Life®. City planners are using Second Life® to design neighborhoods, parks, playgrounds, and even transit systems. The 3D building feature of Second Life® is an efficient way of constructing designs and blueprints from the real world or of getting inspiration from the virtual world to design in the real world without incurring a great expense.

The same meticulous way John Mahon created Dublin in Second Life®, city planners can replicate, edit, and create cityscapes—or cyberscapes—and neighborhoods in Second Life® as part of their real-life constructive planning. Of course, you need to brush up on your 3D building skills, or at least delegate that responsibility to a capable team of builders and designers. However you go about it, remember that Rome wasn't built in a day, nor was it built by one person or based on one idea. Collaborative work projects in Second Life® are one of the richest experiences about the virtual world. There is nothing like it anywhere else.

and organizations are using Second Life® is for the collaborative work process, that is, two or more individuals using their skills and resources to achieve a common goal with others. Noted in the top five most practical ways to use Second Life® is the cost-effective collaborative work ability. Employees of a global company can collaborate on projects in Second Life® without the expense of travel, 3D modeling software, communication software, or other programs. Hundreds of IBM employees from around the globe use Second Life® this way on the dozens of islands they own.

Burning Life, Second Life®'s virtual-world tribute to Burning Man, is yet another great example of collaborative work examples, though carried out in the name of art, music, and subculture dance rituals, the convening of people in a virtual-world destination once a year is remarkable. Dozens of volunteers donate their time and talent to produce a well-choreographed display of art, music, expression, and sound. With hardly any need for direction, seasoned Second Life® avatars gather for the ritualistic lighting of the lamps by volunteer lamp lighters, leading the way to the ceremonious lighting of the man.

As Mitch Kapor discussed in the summer of 2008, though the user-created virtual world is innovative, most big companies cannot yet fathom using it as a replacement to their traditional methods. We do see more and more companies participating in Second Life®, for exploratory and cost-saving measures, but as the virtual world and its communicative abilities are being fine-tuned, we also see employees and businesses utilizing the virtual world currently as an accessory to their current methods of working.

Geographic Coordination

There was a time when conducting business and marketing products to the far reaches of the globe were left up to big companies. It required time, travel, satellite offices, expensive static-filled phone calls, diplomatic relations, visas, passports, and an open mind to customs and cultures. Then the Internet provided a time-saving, cost-effective communication solution with online shopping. Small businesses and entrepreneurs became enabled to easily participate in online communication and global commerce. Pages and pages of Web sites were prepared for the millions of people surfing the Net. Now, instead of pages, places are being prepared for the millions of people teleporting around the virtual world. The 3D virtual world has a geographic value. That is, the virtual world is a place that can be visited (for free) by anyone with an avatar at any time, despite where they are located in the real world.

Having a geographic common ground for your employees located around the country and around the world not only is an efficient form of communication, it provides the sense of presence once achieved exclusively through formal, in-person meetings. The added dimension and immersive quality of Second Life® provide users with the sensation of presence. Although virtual-world gatherings will not replace real-world, face-to-face gatherings, it is the next best thing, and it allows more people to meet not just the executives who travel, but their assistants too. I feel that sense of presence when I work with the Molaskey's team, scheduling and managing events. I feel as if I am with them, though we are thousands of miles apart. In fact, when we met for the first time in real life, there was not a moment of the awkwardness often associated with meeting people for the first time. After collaborating on projects for over two years, we know, trust, and work with each other very well.

For those on the go, working from a remote location, such as an airport, satellite office, or hotel, their ever changing location in real life doesn't stop them from logging into the virtual world of Second Life® and joining their departmental meeting or an interesting lecture or seminar. Even those with work-from-home options can maintain their presence with team members, sharing documents and information with coworkers through the virtual world.

Your virtual-world location not only fosters your company image, it provides a gathering spot for all employees. This can bolster camaraderie and strengthen internal relationships with that sense of presence that conference calls and video presentations just can't accomplish. When you are "there" with others from your company, interacting in a new dimension, you can easily close the geographic gap and virtually erase the miles or oceans between you while you focus on relationship building and collaborative projects.

While working on machinima projects for The Electric Sheep Company in 2007, I participated in a prime example of virtual geographic convergence. We successfully filmed commercials and television segments in Second Life® with avatars whose humans were located in several areas of the world, and yet the avatars were all working in one location. We were simply given a time and a place to be, and we were able to accomplish a great deal.

Though geographic convergence may be solved, time convergence may still be a factor. European-based employees, for example, may find it inconvenient to log into the virtual world at nine in the evening (though that is my favorite time), and Californians may have to log on during their lunch hour to attend a company meeting. But think how far we've come since the days before global business was even possible for so many people. Now, people from any location on Earth can talk with one another for free through the virtual world. When you think of it that way, it's hardly an inconvenience.

Innovative and Efficient

In this era of technology, which includes vast social networking and virtual worlds, communication and global business seem easier and more efficient. That's because innovations like the Internet and 3D virtual worlds are being used in creative and constructive ways, increasing possibilities for business, education, and the quality of life, real and virtual, by doing more for less.

Some of the innovative ways we can expect to see the virtual world shaping up is with the development of user-friendly tools for the average user to navigate and build in Second Life®, making it easier and more enjoyable for more people. Taking it a step further, there is talk of sophisticated depth perception cameras, 3D anatomic modeling, and even geospatial planning that uses 3D cartographic visualization for flight simulation, obviously for the more advanced virtual-world user.

Philip Rosedale has stated his interest in depth perception cameras for use in the virtual world. As he explained, a depth perception camera on your computer that is focused on you in real life can be synchronized with the movement of your avatar so that it gestures as you do in real life, in real time. So, if you're having a conversation with someone in Second Life® while using a depth perception camera, your presence is even stronger. This is still in development but highly anticipated.

Scientists, educators, and skilled builders are finding innovative and efficient ways in which to use Second Life® for the greater good. Several innovative science and research projects are in development at SciLands, the science-centered region of Second Life®.

- The New Media Consortium (NMC), as mentioned in Chapter 8, strongly supports science and education in Second Life®. One of their projects is Research Park, where clinical research is simulated and planned. Students and teachers discuss treatment in an emergency room, for example, playing out situations and protocol. At Research Park, students gain clinical experience in a 3D environment.

- At Genome Island, where genetic experiments are explored in 3D, the public is invited to experiment with science in Second Life®. They perform virtual-world genetic tests demonstrating combinations of genes and traits. They even have a larger-than-life cell that you can go inside, but be warned that your knowledge of science will be tested. The way out of the larger-than-life cell is to properly identify the key components. This is a public destination, encouraging teachers and students to come together on a virtual field trip!

- The National Oceanic and Atmospheric Administration has a map of the United States on display at Science School. This map shows real-time weather conditions using a program from their instruments, loaded onto the Web and into 3D. You can stand in Houston and look across the map to Chicago observing a change in real-time weather conditions.

- Second Nature, the Second Life® home to the science and medicine publication *Nature*, explores 3D molecular structure. They build, categorize and display molecular structure as you might expect a 3D virtual world molecular garden would be. In a sense, it's like a sculpture garden. It's thought provoking. These 3D models serve more than an artistic, meditative retreat for the scientifically minded. They're virtual-world models for teaching and learning.

- Arc Research uses anatomic models, both life-size and several yards larger, to explore the workings of a human body. You can observe a heartbeat and the skeletal system from several points of view, including outside and inside the body. Various scale models are used throughout Second Life® for demonstrative purposes, but they are particularly found in SciLands.

- The solar system has also been replicated in Second Life®, built so that planets orbit in their appropriate sizes and at their appropriate speeds. The V3 Group, mentioned earlier for their work with The Picture Production Company and creation of Silicone Island, created a planetarium with a working 3D model of the solar system.

Travel and Convention Planning

We may see virtual worlds used in the coming years for travel and convention planning. With the ability to create photorealistic, 3D, real-world neighborhoods and city replicas that people can visit for free in Second Life®, travel agencies and convention planners may use Second Life® as a value-added business feature linked from their Web sites.

Coordinating your Web site with your Second Life® site may prove to be a good move, especially for tourism-driven places. When you offer the link from your Web site, you open up a new realm of relationship building with your customers and fascination with tourism. You're presenting and offering a preview of the travel experience and creating an expectation with respect to a destination. (Keeping things in perspective, the virtual world, as I describe it, is never going to *replace* the real world for contact experience, which is so important, but the virtual world puts more things within the reach of more people.)

John Mahon, known in Second Life® as Ham Rambler, owns SL Dublin, a sim in Second Life® that is a good representation of the beloved real city of Dublin, Ireland. He has already proved the value of using Second Life® as a travel destination tool. SL Dublin attracts thousands of virtual-world tourists. Visitors to the virtual-world site are clicking the *Tourism Ireland* billboards strategically placed around SL Dublin, which is linked to the tourism Web site. Tourism Ireland is seeing a tremendous response in traffic to their site, as well as increased sales and interest in Dublin as a result of John's fortuitous virtual-world establishment.

The day will come when you can log into Second Life®, teleport to a virtual-world theme park and convention center, and plan your real-world visit based on your virtual-world experience. It's the know-before-you-go approach to modern vacation planning. Even now it would be possible to use a virtual-world location as a travel-planning tool for conferences, groups, and individuals visiting a real-world destination. From the virtual-world site, you could see where your hotel and conference are in relation to the attractions and events. Perhaps you see that you are too far from where you want to be, whether you have to rent a car, or what attractions are between locations for quick visits. You may also see what entertainment, for example, is scheduled concurrently with your event plans. Travel and convention planners can make that available for you in the virtual world. You can experience the atmosphere of a theme park hotel, and decide whether one is too juvenile or sophisticated for your needs. You can become familiar with the surroundings before you physically arrive at the real-world destination.

This kind of use of the virtual world is an important innovation that tourists, convention hosts, and business planners will appreciate. The theme park will appreciate it too, because this capability has business-adding value, offering a new way to excite visitors with attractions. If my choice came down to the difference between two locations and I were able to take a virtual tour in 3D of one place and not the other, the one with the innovative know-before-you-go travel tour would make a better visual and service impression, therefore getting my business.

The more we explore virtual worlds, the more we see the possibilities and demand for virtual-world representations of real-world destinations. Even if it is just a warmup to a visit, it piques the interest of those remotely considering a visit to someplace; they have established a connection. Hopefully, they are met in the real world with the same positive experiences they find at the virtual-world site. Perhaps assurance they are in the right place would be met with the SL logo, associating the real place with the virtual one. It is an innovative and efficient way of using the virtual world for practical real-world uses.

Everyday Virtual Workspace

Using the virtual world to accomplish everyday work may still seem like a futuristic concept or even a newly angled plea from employees to work from home, but it is a reality that has its merits and is happening now.

While working from my desk at home, I am able to log into Second Life® and interview people for this book; exchange documents, links, and photos; speak on the phone; instant message; manage events at Molaskey's Pub; maintain our Web sites; and copy, scan, fax, mail, and e-mail—all just as I would if I commuted to an office everyday. I have worked at several corporate offices over the years, and I think I get more accomplished in a day by working from home. I am not commuting (up to 90 minutes in some cases) back and forth (or spending money on a train ticket or using gas and miles on my car). I sit at my desk by 8:30 A.M. and finish by 3:30, when my kids get home from school. I often return to my desk in the evening for an hour or two, as needed, but the point is that I can if I need to. I am able to give my attention to my job, my home, and my family with less stress. Besides, I am able to take a lunch break or teatime at my convenience. Balancing home life with work responsibilities has been a challenge, but for many it is now a real possibility.

Using the Internet from home to accomplish work may be more than just a convenience for employees; it may also be an incentive that companies can offer, while scoring points with the environment. When companies offer this flexible schedule to their employees, they are able to retain happier employees without loosing workflow. It may cut down on absenteeism too. Parents with children home from school for illness or inclement weather are able to balance their responsibilities without disrupting their productivity or having to make excuses to their employer. Environmental leaders praise virtual-world work environments because they significantly reduce gas emissions from commuting and wasteful packaging from breakfast and lunch on the go. Virtual-world workspaces are becoming increasingly sensible for both company and employee.

Collaborative Standards

Successful collaboration relies on standards and regulations; that is, everyone needs to use the same measurements, language, and references in order to work collaboratively, not only in Second Life® but throughout the expanding Metaverse. Though Second Life® is a free-form virtual world filled with boundless design and business possibilities that cross over into the real world, unless everyone is using the same standards and calculations, what is built in Second Life® will stay in the virtual world of Second Life®, while other virtual worlds take their own forms.

There is therefore a call for interoperability standards regarding collaborative projects in all virtual worlds, making efficient use of the developing Metaverse. The coordination and synchronistic value of Second Life® and the efficient ways in which to use it are unfurling before us. Although many are experiencing Second Life® for the first time, many others have been hard at work, passionately developing this vast, amazing world with countless possibilities.

Virtual Workspaces

Clear Ink (http://www.clearink.com; blog, http://www.clearnightsky.com) is a successful digital marketing and strategy company that was born in the real world and services the real and virtual worlds. As a digital marketing company, Clear Ink helps clients understand where markets are going. It demonstrates with authority just how prosperous Second Life® can be when properly used to its fullest advantage. Led by Steve Nelson, Clear Ink is using Second Life® in innovative and collaborative ways.

Nelson, also known as SL™-Kiwini Oe, and Second Life® architect Jon Brouchoud are collaborating on a big project. It involves a global company that will establish their headquarters in Second Life®. It will be used for conferencing and creating a multiple collaborative platform where employees will perform their everyday jobs on real-time projects, with employees and customers around the globe. This is the type of business model that may convince other real-world business to use the virtual world of Second Life® as a platform for their daily business practices.

According to Steve, "These work collaborations will bring together teams that span multiple real-life geographic locations and bring them into one virtual HQ area." He notes that for this project, they have experimented with collaborative tools such as a Print to Second Life® feature for Mac OS X, which can print to a Second Life® printer so that avatars can all see the output (see http://clearnightsky.com/node/371 for Steve's detailed explanation).

BUSINESS STRATEGIES

10.

Business
Relationships

Rome wasn't built in a day, and it certainly wasn't built by one person. Even in a digital world where everything is built by keystrokes and software, people need to rely on one another to reach their business goals. Historically, we have based our relationships on telecommunications, correspondence, pages on the Internet, and, of course, real-world encounters. In recent years, relationships in the virtual world are being recognized for their expressive, personable, and meaningful bonds. They are bridging the gap between the Internet and real-world encounters. This is a new type of relationship, writing the latest page in business and communication history.

The story is often told about persons who join Second Life® just to explore and to learn. After talking with other people and seeing the thriving businesses blossoming in-world, they can't help but be inspired and excited about the opportunities they see and the ideas they have. Rather than sit idly by, they find virtual-world jobs or develop a Second Life® business, usually with the people they meet in-world.

What Makes Second Life® Relationships Work

The most important part of business building in Second Life® is relationship building. Compatibility is an important component of the success of your business.

Whether it is in the real world or Second Life®, relationships are built on respect and trust. From there, they develop into more complex levels of understanding and rhythm. These symbiotic relationships work so well because a virtual-world relationship shares essential components with a real-world relationship, fusing high-tech methods with organic personality:

- Respect

- Trust

- Enjoyment

- Shared goals and complementary skills

- Rhythm and synchronicity

Respect

You accept one another for how you present yourselves. The virtual world does a good job of breaking prejudicial barriers. In the virtual world, you choose how you want to present yourself, and so does everyone else. You can have any color skin, hair, or eyes you choose; in fact, my friend Gilly often wears celestial skin, dotted with sparkling stars! You can be human or animal, or even robotic if you want. The point is that it is your choice to make. You can experiment with your appearance, and alter it at will for different purposes. This kind of representation reminds us that you can go beyond your physical appearance and express your comprehensive personality. I find that the more experimental, outrageous, and personable an avatar is, the more respect they receive from the community. Virtual-world relationships are not about race, gender, age, disability, or other discriminations seen in the real world. In Second Life®, how you present yourself is your choice. In my opinion, all people deserve respect until they give you reason otherwise.

Trust

Trusting relationships can be successfully formed in the virtual world. Trust in the virtual world means being reliable. You can detect people's competence and commitment not only in the first encounter, but by spending enough time with them. You can gather their tone, manners, professionalism, and intellect by how they regularly present themselves through their avatar, and they, of course, can do the same with you. Earning trust with a virtual-world avatar is just as important as in the real world.

Enjoyment

Enjoyment is one of the top five reasons why SL people like being with one another. In an interactive social world, a pleasant personality is as important as any skill you have. You don't have to be the most talkative person in the room to express your personality. Simply making a few comments at the right time can be gratifying. Your physical attributes and gestures will also speak for you.

Your avatar can be programmed with an animation override, which is a programmed animation that promotes more human qualities for your avatar. You can customize the way you walk, sit, or stand to be less rigid than the generic avatar. Gestures are the motions you give your avatar, and they may accompany a programmed chat line or audio clip, such as the sound of applause or a quote from a movie, like "Stella!" These are small, jovial reminders that we are in a creative virtual world. They're fun and easy to perform. These so-called character accessories are extremely valuable in demonstrating or enhancing one's personality.

Shared Goals and Complementary Skills

Successful business relationships often achieve balance by having shared goals and different skills. When you pair up with other professionals to reach a business goal, you rely on one another for specific skills and qualities. In the Molaskey group, Katydid and Apple, the primary group owners, are both graphics and marketing professionals. Their skills, personalities, and styles are different, but their common goal is to bring Molaskey's Pub to the forefront of the virtual-world social and music scene. They have a great working relationship.

Rhythm and Synchronicity

Virtual-world relationships develop rhythm and synchronicity, just as real-world relationships do. You go the same pace. When you get to know someone in the virtual world, it is because you are both logging on at approximately the same time. Perhaps you are within the same time zone and your real-life schedules are similar. If you have similar interests, you may also be making the same effort to be at the same events, converging at the same time and place. When you find a comfortable rhythm with the people you meet, and you find them to have the qualities of being a friend or even business associate, don't hesitate to reach out to them. This is a world that's all about social interaction.

Adding a Friend

Once you have established an introduction with those you meet, you may need to retain a relationship. Adding a person to your friends list adds to the ease and convenience of communication. Doing this is as easy as opening a person's profile and clicking on the Add Friend button. If a person is already on your friend's list, that button will be gray. If not, it is highlighted and ready to click.

There are several ways of opening up a person's profile. First, you can right-click on the avatar if it is nearby. Right-clicking on it brings up the pie menu that offers Profile as well as Add Friend. Be careful not to click on Add Friend if all you intend is to discretely look at their profile. Next thing you know, you have offered friendship to a person you didn't actually mean to. I have done this. It happens. I remain friends with Lib Nilsson for that very reason. Although it is possible to delete a friend, Lib and I had a good laugh (at my expense), so we decided to keep the friendship. I have to say, though, Lib has a great sense of humor.

Another way of opening a profile is by entering a name in the People section of the search engine. This may prove to be a safer way to research a person without erroneously befriending.

Do:

- Ask permission of the person you want to add to your friends list. Be polite.

- If someone offers you friendship and you are not willing to give your friendship, have a response prepared like, "I don't accept friendships that quickly" or, more humorously, "Not on the first meeting!"

- Keep notes of when you meet a person and how you know them or how they know you. This can be done in their profile in the My Notes tab. This is an area of every profile just for you, as sort of a cheat sheet to keep track of all you meet. No one else can see your prompt notes about a person in the My Notes section of a profile.

- Consider the human behind the avatar, not just the avatar. Almost everyone has a busy real life, not just Second Life®. Allow reasonable response time from others when you contact them.

Don't:

- Don't randomly offer friendship to people. This is largely considered intrusive, and your friendship won't mean much of anything to anyone.

- Don't be afraid to turn down friendships or to delete friends as necessary. There are times when we realize that we have taken on more than we can handle; just don't be rude about it.

- Don't subject everyone on your friends list to spam or randomly offer a teleport for every sales pitch or party you have. Save that for your group. Some friends want to remain just acquaintances, not become buddies.

Point of Trust

Adding a friend is common practice. Knowing when to trust that friend with certain information, such as phone numbers and family information, brings a trusting friendship onto a different level. You wouldn't give out personal information to strangers, so don't let your guard down in the virtual world. My rule of thumb: Release only information to others that may be publicly found on your resume, such as your name, e-mail, and the like. Don't freely give the names of your children, income, or any deeply personal information. Use common sense.

As people meet online, it is usually a good idea to protect your personal information until you reach a point of trust through an actual conversation, Web site reference, and other credentials. When someone displays elusive, erratic behavior or uses vulgarities, flags go up, and I remain reserved about disclosing any detailed information about myself. I rely on my senses when meeting people. When I meet other professionals through referencing Web sites and similar means, I feel more comfortable about sharing my information, such as what I do for a living, geographic location, and so on. For those who truly need to speak with me, I offer my telephone number. This is the kind of information found on your resume anyway and should be shared with potential business partners.

How to Read a Profile

A person's profile can offer plenty of information. The first page shows the avatar's picture, the groups it belongs to, the date it entered Second Life®, the partner (if any), and a few free-form words.

By clicking on the tabs, you can go deeper into the profile, clicking on the link to the related Web site, following their general interests, languages spoken, favorite places around Second Life®, classified ads they posted, and selected real-life info. Profiles are completed and maintained by residents, so by providing certain information, they are allowing you an insight into their Second Life® goals and persona. The Second Life® profile is not exactly a professional resume; it's more of a definition of character.

If I see a person uses a professional portrait and has filled out most or all of the profile information, I know that person is an active participant, tending to details and appearance. If most of the profile is blank or it seems dated, they are likely uncommitted, are not detail oriented, and need help with their virtual-world skills. Reading a profile can be a pleasure or a disappointment.

A person's name is the gateway to personality. Since Second Life® names are selected by residents, you can instantly tell something about them by the names they chose. Apple MacKay, for instance, was chosen as a dedication to Jay's beloved computer, Apple Macintosh, but also for the symbol of knowledge, the apple. Jay is a mentor and a knowledgeable source for many, so his chosen name is fitting. Other names, like Katydid Something, may suggest creativity, or Nasus Dumart, which is somewhat enigmatic (Nasus is Susan in reverse). Avatar names offer a clue to a person's character, and that is why we suggest careful consideration of your chosen Second Life® name.

You can reach a few character conclusions just by seeing the groups of which a person is affiliated. You are allowed to have up to 25 group memberships per avatar. This may seem like plenty, but they fill up fast. If a person is an educator, party animal, techie, artist, or networking business type, it will show through their group affiliations.

Joining a Group

Groups have two ways of enrolling members. In open enrollment, anyone just opens the group profile and clicks the button to join. The other way is by invitation only. When you join a group, you can expect some notices to be sent to you in the form of a pop-up window on your screen while you're logged on. When you are logged off Second Life®, the notices go to your e-mail. Be warned: Some groups are very active, sending many notices. You do, however, have the option to not receive instant notices.

How Involved Do You Want to Be?

Groups have three levels of membership: Everyone, Officer, and Owner. Are you joining a group to actively participate or just for the affiliation? Most groups do not require involvement, allowing you simply to participate as a basic member, but if you are more inclined to take the lead on projects, you may be better suited as an officer or owner.

An officer is given the authority to manage the group, such as to add or ban residents, send notices to the group, and place objects on the land. The owners have the overall power, with unrestricted authority, to manage the group. In the Molaskey's group, we have two co-owners, five officers, and the remaining 550 members (or so) are in the Everyone category. In our group, the officers and owners create, manage, and host events. Although this is not a full-time job for any of us, we are all committed to the plans we make with the group and carry them out to the best of our ability. Basic group members receive event notices, participate in group chat, and drop in on concerts and parties at their leisure.

Joining a group presents many opportunities to network. You may consider volunteering your time and skills for groups in which you are sincerely interested. Not only do you have the exposure as a leader and organizer, you gain valuable experience doing something you love. Networking through professional associations, hobby groups, educational groups, and social situations creates strong relationships.

Because Second Life® is relatively new, most of the business in Second Life® consists of start-up companies, where the entrepreneurs do most of the work or rely on volunteers during the launch of their businesses. Also, many established companies in Second Life® are hiring group managers. If you exhibit exceptional potential using Second Life® by leading a group and events, you could be considered a virtual-world commodity and presented with a job offer. Being on the group payroll presents a different kind of commitment. There are two kinds of jobs in Second Life® that I know of: those that pay in real dollars and those that pay in Linden money. The real money contract is usually an agreement between a consultant and a client. The Linden arrangement is for providing a virtual-world service such as hosting events for a group. These jobs are taken as seriously as any part-time job in the real world. It requires a commitment to a schedule and competence in knowing how to handle situations and engaging conversations.

Interacting with Your Group

Notices and group chat reach every member of a group instantly. Group notices arrive in the form of a drop-down window with your group insignia and message. These notices are usually created and sent by authorized members of a group, such as managers. Group chat, on the other hand, is an instant message that appears in the chat line of every member of the group. For some groups, that message reaches thousands of members simultaneously!

This can be taken two ways—as useful or annoying. Any member of a group can instigate chat with the entire group. It is properly used when members of the group reach out to other members for help or information relevant to the group. Sometimes this feature is abused with spam, which is (annoying) cheap, unauthorized advertising through e-mail and instant messaging. A person may open group chat with a quick blurb and a link to a promotion unrelated to the group, knowing they are reaching hundreds and potentially thousands of people simultaneously. After spamming a group, a member is usually given a verbal warning or immediately ejected from the group.

People join our group to be informed of our events. When we have concerts at the Pub and want to remind the group and offer a teleport, we use group chat. We begin with a comment like, "Join us on Bonfire Beach for an unforgettable performance by Skinny Shepherd starting NOW!" That kind of comment prompts commentary from members, such as, "Send me a ride!" and "Me too!" or "Hiya Apple! Haven't seen you in a while—be right there!" Banter ensues and carries on for several minutes between those who choose to chime in. For the several hundred other members reading along, it can be ignored, and the group chat window closed. By using the group chat, we engage our group with relevant topics, resulting in an enriching conversation and getting several attendees to events that they might not have known about.

Just as you have individual relationships, you also have dynamic group relationships. Some of the more active groups maintain lively conversations with all members, all kept in the context of the group's topics. Members can be located anywhere in Second Life® and receive information and participate in a conversation with their group.

Forming Secondary Groups

A group may focus on one main topic while spawning other areas of interest, which evolve. Recently, I formed a group called Pub Crawlers and invited other quality pubs of Second Life® to participate in a virtual Pub Crawl, for fun and publicity. This couldn't be done under the Molaskey's Pub group because of the number of other pubs involved.

Think closely of your evolving needs before forming a new group. It is easy to form a new group, but don't expect the same people from one of your groups to join

Second Life® Groups

Each of the following groups and individuals mentioned is an example of the variety of relationships successfully maintained in the virtual world.

- Astrin Few and his fellow musician friend, Flaming Moe, formed the Live Music Enthusiasts group, which builds the relationships among musicians of all genres, their fans, and the venue owners. The Live Music Enthusiast group was formed with the sole intent of announcing live music performances 10 minutes before taking the stage, offering group members a SLurl™ to go directly to the show at the click of a mouse. This is an ideal model of the successful use of targeted group communication. This kind of communication became widely accepted by both the musicians and the venue owners, helping to define the live music scene in Second Life®.

- Metanomics, the business and education group in Second Life®, is led by Prof. Robert Bloomfield, of The Johnson School at Cornell University. Every week, Metanomics members meet to discuss virtual-world business topics and trends. The members often carry the conversation into group chat, where it takes a more personal turn. I know I have become more familiar with names and personalities this way than by seeing the avatars from the group in other situations. My relationship with the group is much the same as any relationship with an individual, only the Metanomics group consists of over a thousand individuals. As a whole, they represent a category of business and a group of professionals.

- Artropolis is an artist colony formed by real-world artist Jeffrey Lipsky, known in Second Life® as Filthy Fluno. Artists exhibit their work in an interactive environment while collaborating with one another during the process. Patrons know where to find professional artists in Second Life® by establishing a relationship with members of the Artropolis group.

- Mac Users Group is a group of Mac users in Second Life® that uses group chat for questions and help from fellow Macintosh devotees. Someone may simply ask, "How do I . . . ?" and several expert users will offer help and valuable resources.

your other groups. With a limit of 25 simultaneous groups per avatar, they max out fast. People carefully consider the groups in which they belong, often having to leave one to join another.

Professionalism in In-World Relationships

Nowhere else in the universe do you encounter as much diversity, personal expression, outrageous situations, or odd encounters as in the virtual world. It's virtually indescribable to anyone who has not experienced it first-hand. All silliness and oddity aside, more than half of what goes on in the virtual world represents valuable business, so a good measure of professionalism is still expected.

When I was granted an interview in Second Life® with Grady Booch of IBM, there was no doubt in my mind that this was a conservative encounter. My avatar wore a suit, neatly tied black hair, and no bling. I was prepared in real life with a notebook and questions as if this were a real-life encounter. There was a moderator, who greeted me at the specific time of the interview, on location at IBM in Second Life®. A few minutes later, Grady's avatar arrived, and we three sat to talk for an hour. At the end of the hour, we stood up, made conclusive remarks, such as, "Thank you for your time. Let's keep in touch," and we ended the meeting by saying "Good-bye" and teleporting away. The corporate protocol during this meeting was the same in Second Life® as in real life.

On the other hand, one of the more outrageous meetings I have attended was the telecommunications subcommittee hearing, which took place at a real-world session of the U.S. Congress. The meeting I attended was streamed into the virtual world, where dozens of Second Life® avatars looked on, feverishly chatting with excitement in the open forum. In the real world, Philip Rosedale, Dr. Colin Parris, Dr. Larry Johnson, and Ms. Susan Tenby proficiently presented Second Life® and all its potential to the telecommunications subcommittee in Washington, D.C. Meanwhile, behind the scenes in the virtual world, I watched as outrageous avatars crowded the floor of a virtual representation of a congressional office, with humorous and sometimes irreverent comments and gestures. It was near blasphemy. It was also one of the most memorable meetings I had the honor of attending.

The Importance of Being Open-Minded in Second Life®

When you meet people representing themselves through out-of-the ordinary avatars, remember to see someone for the content of their character. Creative expression is encouraged in the virtual world, but you are expected to remain in context with your environment in certain situations.

When Gender and Race Boundaries Are Crossed

When people create avatars, they are deciding on how to represent themselves. Don't be surprised, as I was, to learn that many avatars are created specifically to cross gender and racial barriers. I had considered profiling someone in this book for their expertise in a particular area of business. When I met them, by chance, at the Second Life® Community Convention, I decided to give the business a different mention. To my complete surprise, the SL "she" was a real life "he"! I will not disclose who the person is, but I will tell you that the cross-gender decision was strategic. He is proud that his success in Second Life® is as a business-driven female avatar. On the flip side, some women find success in Second World as a business-driven male.

Do's and Don'ts of Professionalism in Second Life®

Do:

- Know when to maintain your real-world professional manners in the virtual world and when they can be relaxed.

- Let your human side show through your avatar. Enjoy the creative atmosphere of the virtual world without letting your professional guard down.

- Demonstrate personality and professionalism equally.

Don't:

- Carry on a business conversation in open chat. Be sure to use private chat for conversations between yourself and other key individuals. Hold a private conference if you need to include more than one person in a private conversation.

- Say anything you wouldn't want on the record. Conversations in chat are on the record.

Navigating Sight-Unseen Worries

In Second Life®, where a majority of people work together without meeting in person, there is an understanding unlike any in real life. You enter into relationships sight unseen, relying more on instinct and impressions than physical evidence.

Most of the successful business start-ups in Second Life® are a result of relationships formed on line, sight unseen. Michael Pinkerton, from the staffing company Metaverse Mod Squad, stated, "This is a bold new business practice, indeed, but it's not uncommon for business partners to collaborate 'site unseen' and it certainly proves possible."

The Molaskey's Pub team, with the exception of Jay and me, worked sight unseen during the first two years of our online existence. During that time, we built the Pub, formed our group of over 500 members, planned and managed weekly events, and developed deep relationships based on mutual respect, a sense of humor, patience, online and real-world skills, and an understanding of one another's personality. As a result of our online relationships, professional practices, and commitment to Molaskey's Pub, we have built one of the most respected and admired live music venues and social destinations in all of Second Life®. We're very proud of that.

Second Life® business partners and group dynamics are unique relationships largely established sight unseen, and yet these relationships are strong and diverse. Treat your virtual-world relations as you would someone in real life. Remember that behind every avatar is a person. We usually rely on our sensory system where sight, sound, feel, smell, and taste usually guide our instincts, so establishing business relationships in the virtual world may seem like a leap of faith, but there are many examples of how they instinctively work.

When Worlds Collide

When we first started learning about it, we did not discuss Second Life® with anyone in the real world. We weren't doing anything wrong; it's just that the virtual world was too outrageous to describe to those not already in it. I often said it was like trying to describe the Internet to someone in 1979. For several months, while we were learning about it, Second Life® was a closed subject to most of our real-world friends and family, sparing us odd looks and concern. Once we were comfortable with the virtual world of Second Life® and why we were spending so much time there, talking about it with people in real life became easier. In fact, it became a favorite subject.

I know several people from my real life who now have Second Life® avatars. With the advantage of knowing their real-life and online personalities, I gain further insight, as I guess they do of me. In the real world, we may talk about our children, global concerns, and even light politics, but in the virtual world, it's about exploring the world from our home, unfolding (and pursuing) a broad spectrum of interests, and developing an online personality in the interim.

Keeping the real world and the virtual world separate may be the choice for those using Second Life® for recreational use. It can be very hard to describe the virtual world to those in your real world. Your better judgment may tell you not to explain that you are friends with dozens of people from around the world, all with crazy names that you have never met, or that you spend time with them in fantastic places as an avatar in a 3D online world. Although you are creating a fabulous life online, your credibility with people of the real world may be on *the* line.

Blending your real life with your virtual one, however, can be advantageous when you are using Second Life® for business and networking. Second Life® is an extremely effective and popular way of networking, so telling people you're in Second Life® certainly results in getting you some attention. In fact, if you haven't already,

Taking the Leap

The Metaverse Mod Squad was formed by a group of professionals in Second Life who have a unique background in online business, message board moderation, law, security, and social networking. Their skills and personality came through their avatars, in conversations, and in their style of working. In fact, they worked "site" unseen for several months during the start of their business. Michael Pinkerton, Metaverse Mod Squad's COO, mentioned that they met in real life only two days before the convention where I met them. Although they were able to launch a profitable business with an impressive brand and client base, it was done entirely based on their virtual-world dynamics. They knew, based on professional history and compatibility online, that they could work together. They had a great idea, as well as the right professionals in the right medium at the right time, so they did not hesitate to make their move and start a business together.

The Metaverse Mod Squad offers professional staffing services in Second Life and beyond. They find avatars who can offer product demonstrations and who can be greeters, event hosts, children's moderators, entertainers, and security personnel. The people hired by Metaverse Mod Squad and other virtual-world companies for temporary jobs around Second Life are typically hired sight unseen. They are seasoned Second Life residents who are placed based on their virtual-world abilities, personality, and professionalism. It doesn't matter how people look, sound, or behave in their real lives, as long as they look, chat, and behave in a professional manner according to their virtual-world job descriptions.

you will begin to see resumes, business cards, and other profile information include virtual-world names and associations.

Whether you use Second Life® as a personal and private escape from the real world or as a blend of virtual- and real-world professional opportunities, discussing your life online with others is a choice only you can make.

11.

Marketing 2.0

Marketing and selling your product, services, business, and brand in Second Life® require new methods of marketing that mix advanced technology with simple interaction.

Customers may already be familiar with your television, print, or Internet presence, but Second Life® offers a whole new platform with its own marketing potential. In Second Life®, you have the opportunity to engage regular customers and potential new customers with 3D simulation, by creating an attractive virtual-world experience, and through individual interaction.

In Second Life®, often referred to as Internet 2.0, marketing methods are being developed that combine the Internet's ability to inform with the virtual world's capacity to simulate real-world experiences. This so-called Marketing 2.0 is about adapting to the requirements of the audience and the technological medium, rather than assuming either will support traditional marketing methods. Steve Nelson of Clear Ink observes that most clients are still looking for the number of viewers to enter their virtual-world site. It is hard to convince clients that it's not about numbers in the virtual world. He has found that people jump on the Second Life® bandwagon without knowing enough about what they are doing. He refers to the Gartner Group Hype Cycle and advises marketers not to give up, but rather to understand the medium and keep the activity going, even if they're not getting the millions of eyeballs they were hoping for.

While attracting a thousand Second Life® visitors to your site a month shows you're doing something right, getting them to stay and interact with your products or service people is the real art of marketing in-world. As Dr. Colin Parris points out, when people visit, "they spend a good hour there, testing your products, connecting with your brand, keeping away from your competitor." This allows you to double or triple your traffic and create a word-of-mouth buzz.

So go ahead—create a lasting impression. Make an *interactive* global medium work for you.

Do:

- Know what you want from your Second Life® presence. Are you using it as a fresh market for an existing product, to launch a new product, for sales presentations, to hold meetings, or for community interaction? Prepare a marketing plan that clearly states your objective.

- Support your Second Life® presence by including it in your real-world marketing material. Offer real-world audiences your SLurl, send them invitations to Second Life events, and post photos from your events in-world.

- Alert the media with press releases and video news releases.

- Create virtual-world marketing giveaways that avatars want, such as novelty items and costumes with your logo on them.

- Blog about your Second Life® business as part of the online community. Build a presence in the blogger community.

Don't:

- Create a space bigger than you need. Social media like Second Life® are based on interaction, starting with simple conversations. If you build a cavernous location as your landing spot with the intent of impressing people, the opportunity for visitors to engage one another may be lost in the space between them.

- Just rehash traditional marketing methods. Invest as much creativity and expression in your marketing materials as you invest in your avatar and building site.

Interaction: What a Concept!

The key to successfully establishing a virtual-world marketing strategy is not with impressions, viewers, or hits, but with interaction. Some companies found that out the hard way, having set up a presence in Second Life® during the height of the hype without knowing exactly how to use it. Steve Nelson, a specialist in digital marketing at Clear Ink, described this phenomenon: "I think there were some expectations set [in

Second Life® Marketing Maestros

Sibley Verbeck (http://blogs.electricsheepcompany.com/sibley), owner and founder of The Electric Sheep Company (ElectricSheepCompany.com), has valuable first-hand experience with the Second Life® Hype Cycle. Organizations such as CBS, Sundance Channel, Pontiac, Bantam Dell, Ben and Jerry's, Reuters, the NBA, the Swedish Embassy, and others have turned to The Electric Sheep Company in Second Life® for quality virtual-world content, virtual-world services, and broadcast machinima.

Sibley and The Electric Sheep Company have made their virtual mark on the world by exploring the interactive branding and marketing possibilities in Second Life®. Giff Constable, the chief operating officer of Electric Sheep, states they "help corporations understand and utilize the virtual world," providing companies and their consumers with a "more enjoyable experience." And through a combination of expertise and trial and error, they have contributed to the development of Marketing 2.0.

As a former chief scientist of StreamSage, Inc. and Comcast Online, Sibley formed The Electric Sheep Company in Second Life® in 2005 with a handful of employees. They rose to the top, nearly too fast during 2006 and 2007, by providing clients with impressive structures, professionally designed content, software development, and staffing services. They have branched out to other virtual worlds, such as There.com and MTV's virtual world. Sibley is able to project the direction of technology, the market, pop culture, and virtual-world abilities. Along with Sibley's expertise, a dedicated staff of 3D architects, designers, scripters, directors, producers, back-end personnel, and miscellaneous staff have made The Electric Sheep Company a success.

2007] based on readings of the population that were unrealistic, especially for those who thought this was a marketing medium." Companies applied traditional marketing methods using click-throughs and message boards. Then they went back to the real world and waited. Their Second Life® marketing plan was ineffective because they didn't understand Second Life® as a real-time interactive online platform and expected traditional online consumer activity.

Your brand name is not enough to stand alone in the virtual world. You cannot take a field of dreams approach: Even if you build it, they may not come. This is an interactive medium. Second Life® residents represent a whole new demographic, a new audience that wants your genuine involvement as much as you want theirs.

Go Where the Avatars Are

Take the interactive potential of Second Life® off your campus and out onto the virtual world. Don't wait for avatars to come to you—go to them!

What if your Web site could search for customers who were surfing the Net and lure them in with friendly, personable conversation? Does that sound preposterous? Your Web site is an inanimate page holder that just sits there and waits for people to visit and get information about your business. In Second Life®, your avatar is a mobile representation of your company. You can go to events at established venues that are already attracting the crowds while wearing your company group tag.

One of the best ways to bring your marketing message to avatars is to sponsor community events and well-attended concerts. Most established live music venues, like Molaskey's Pub, will team up with you. Organizations like the American Cancer Society and production companies like The SL Shakespeare Company (SL Shakespeare.com) have sponsorship programs available.

You can also expand your role by supporting the community events that coincide with your business through associations or related educational and nonprofit work. By doing so, you are building a relationship with your target market,

Popular Avatar Destinations

Where do avatars hang out? Where can companies reap the benefits of interacting with avatars?

- Molaskey's Pub has several events a week. We generate steady traffic, which is the envy of many high-priced corporate sites in Second Life® on a mission to penetrate the virtual-world market. Companies come to us to tap into our ability to generate traffic, and we provide them with promotional material to connect with the virtual-world community.

- SL Dublin created an entire neighborhood of the real-world city in Ireland. They created real-world attractions, such as Trinity College, Guinness Brewery, and The Blarney Stone Pub, in the virtual world. The work in building a virtual-world office, participating in community events, and generating traffic is already done. It's such an immersive, attractive destination that real-world companies are gladly paying rent on the virtual-world property, seeing results even in Web site hits.

- The SL Shakespeare Company is one of the finest establishments in Second Life®, not only for their incredible digital structures, organization, and professional manner, but also for being one of the most highly intelligent performing troupes I have come across. Their virtual-world performances are no less involved than any real-world counterpart. Ina Centaur, SL Shakespeare's artistic director and executive producer, holds sponsors in high honor, recognizing their support with Shakespearian titles: Pennies Patron, Galleries' Patron, Preshow Encore, Bard's Muse, Thespian's Idol, and Monarch's Will. The highest honor is Enterprise Benefactor. The sponsoring effort is no different from supporting real-life arts.

not just catching their attention for a shallow impression. People will see you are investing in their community and supporting their interests, and they will support you in turn.

Through sponsorship, you are reaching more people than you could on your own, establishing a relationship with the market, and supporting the community—all of which always weighs in your favor. Use the interactive abilities of the virtual world to connect with your market and embed yourself in the community.

Do:

- Take the time to attend several different events around Second Life®. There are live music performances, city destinations, stage performances, art galleries, lectures, parties, and competitive game events, to name a few.

- Establish a business relationship with the venues that attract regular crowds.

- Sponsor events at busy venues.

- Use an automated chat, when allowed, during events that say, "[Your Company] is a proud sponsor of the [Venue Name] concert series."

- Set up a poster by the stage where people can see snapshots from today's and past events.

- Provide posters with a click-through to a special section of your Web site that is loaded with virtual-world event snapshots. People will want to see the snapshots and your Web site.

- On the flip side, people visiting your Web site will take an interest in the snapshots of the virtual world and click-through to the virtual world, landing at your office or store location.

- Have a virtual-world host attend sponsored events on behalf of your company and engage the crowd. Have another at your virtual office or store to greet visitors during peak periods. These virtual-world employees can be from your existing staff, trained to use Second Life®, or you can hire a Second Life® resident for a few hours at a time, paid in Linden dollars. (Event hosts in SL are paid about L$300–L$500 an hour—about US$2. Well worth it.)

- Create your own interesting series of virtual-world events (once you are established with your target market) that highlight or demonstrate your company, product, or service.

Don't:

- Expect people to go to your corporate Web site or virtual-world site unless you give them reason to.

- Try to hard-sell your product or virtual-world presence by being persistent or overly chatty about it. That approach will backfire. Conversations tend to flow from topic to topic in open forums. If you keep coming back to your product and your business without prompts from others, you will be considered rude.

Hosting Events on Your Property

Bringing traffic to your site is where the challenge, the fun, and the opportunities lie. On Web sites, potential customers visit for a few minutes—if you're lucky. In Second Life®, the goal is to engage them for a much longer time.

Hundreds of parties and concerts are happening in Second Life® at any given time, but what draws a crowd are the people and the activities on offer. At Molaskey's we have first-rate musicians playing regularly. They bring their following, fans, or groupies. We host many holiday parties and themed birthday parties. We have special events like the Pub Crawl and chess tournaments. These are the kinds of events and social mixers that people want to attend.

Here are a few tips for hosting events on your site.

Do:

- Create clear and simple signage about your event, and place the signs in high-traffic areas.

- Promote your event through your Web site or blog.

- List your event for free on the Second Life® events listing (http://.Secondlife .com/Events).

- Announce your event on extended social networks such as Plurk, Facebook, Google Groups, Eventful, and the like.

- Create a SLurl (a Second Life® link) that brings people directly to the event. Do this by standing in the desired landing spot and opening Map at the bottom of your screen. Touch Copy SLurl™. Close the map. Then go into your group chat and paste it. It becomes highlighted as a link to the landing spot you just created.

- Use your friends list and groups to send out invitations.

- Before your guests arrive, check your sim for lag issues caused by heavy and overbearing scripts. Lag causes slow performance and a less than de-sirable experience. Correct problems as needed. If necessary, someone from Linden Lab will assist you.

- Provide entertainment by way of a DJ or live musician.

- Provide animations and costumes that avatars can use to fully experience your event, like dance moves and movie character costumes and props.

- Have interesting details and activities on your site, such as a photo album, artifacts, or even an ice skating rink.

Don't:

- Expect people to come just because you invite them.

- Rely on the streamed Internet radio as your musical entertainment. It's akin to putting the radio on for a party, commercials and all.

- Be dismayed by low turnout. Some of the best parties are with just ten people. Try again and again.

Attracting a Crowd

Having a virtual-world site doesn't mean that an avatar should just sit there all day and field questions from people who happen to stroll (or fly) by. Residents need a reason to search your company, product, or service and to teleport to your site. Be expressive and inventive. Nothing is more humdrum to a virtual-world audience than to see the same ole thing from the real world. Give them the ability to do, see, and experience what the virtual world can offer that the real world may not. Have celebrity appearances, an educational lecture series, mixed reality events. Present unique opportunities that allow people to have encounters through your virtual-world site that would be otherwise out of their reach.

Novelty Architecture

I once found a real-world communications company that was experimenting with Second Life®. The firm bought an island and developed a campus with expensive-looking landscaping details, complete with a guardhouse and gate. There were several glass-enclosed buildings with elevators and offices. It was a perfect copy of a fancy corporate park. But what baffled me was that with all the possibilities in the virtual world, they replicated a cubical-filled office environment. I recall leaving there in a hurry.

Despite your corporate environment in the real world, use the virtual world to create something enticing. It is just as easy to build novelty architecture in Second Life® as it is to recreate a standard corporate office.

As Giff Constable of The Electric Sheep Company said, "This is not a cookie-cutter operation." What works in the real world may not, or will not, work in the virtual world. What really excites the virtual-world audience is creativity. Be abstract to a comfortable degree.

If you're a well-known franchise coffee shop in the real world, don't replicate your store with a four-point structure in the virtual world. Instead, create a building that replicates, say, a two-story to-go cup of coffee with your famous logo on the side. Inside, avatar/customers can get a steaming hot cup of coffee. Serving coffee in the virtual world may be for the avatars, but you can use the site to list real-world locations of your stores, franchise opportunities, and a list of events sponsored in the real and virtual worlds.

Scope Cleaver, Second Life® conceptual designer and architect, is booked well into the future. He takes virtual-world design to the virtual-world boundary, if there is one. When you can create structures in the virtual world that defy real-world laws of physics, gravity, and practicality, why not explore such opportunities to the fullest?

If you are a snowboard company building a Second Life® presence, perhaps you could consider a traditional slope-side lodge, complete with ski lift for a product demo. If you are a deep-sea diving company, the real-world prevents you from having a shop underwater where you can better demonstrate your products. Now is your chance.

Iconic structures, historic roadside stops, and architecture from the Golden Age of Hollywood are good examples of the type of architecture that is finding a revival in Second Life® because it is appealing, creative, and fun.

Whatever you decide as your virtual-world structure—whether abstract, novelty, traditional, historical, skybox, or underwater—the point is to make it interesting and visually appealing. Such structures photograph well, and snap-happy avatars will share their photos.

Celebrity Appearances

Nothing draws a crowd like a celebrity. Although I am certain celebrities are walking among us as plain ole avatars, as soon as someone is identified as a celebrity, wearing the actual name issued by Linden Lab, there is near pandemonium. Maybe it isn't like the Beatles arriving in America, but there is a noteworthy upswing of energy.

For example, I attended a book reading by best-selling author Dean Koontz in March 2007. The event was held at the Bantam Dell bookstore in Second Life®. The Electric Sheep Company promoted the event, providing several sims to handle the anticipated crowds. The interview and book reading were streamed live onto screens on several locations while group chat provided instant commentary and questions for the author through a moderator. Hundreds of people were able to attend this one-hour appearance, while the author sat comfortably and read from a desk in an office.

Celebrity appearances don't have to be on such a grand scale. They can be just promotional appearances, charity fund-raising, political activism, or a meet-and-greet or photo opportunity. In any situation, you can generate excitement in the virtual world with a celebrity appearance or two.

The same is true of a lecture series. Invite experts to speak on topics relevant to your product and business. A person doesn't have to be a celebrity to draw a crowd, just interesting, knowledgeable, and skilled at public speaking.

Mixed Reality Events

Having an event that takes place in both the real world and in the virtual world draws a crowd. It is an interesting concept to merge both worlds, and the Swedish embassy in Washington, D.C., has successfully done this. In the lobby of the real-world embassy, visitors were captured on camera as they peered into the virtual world, provided by a large plasma screen. Concurrently, avatars at the embassy in Second Life® saw the real-world visitors and were also captured on camera, which was streamed into the real world. Essentially, they could wave to each other in real time. This multidimensional phenomenon drew a steady stream of traffic and some publicity.

Some musicians will perform mixed reality events. None of them uses the high-tech equipment needed to photograph both worlds simultaneously, as the Swedish embassy was able to do, but they play for a real and a virtual audience at the same time. This is done by bringing their laptop on stage and connecting to Second Life® during their performance. Only the most skilled musicians can manage the multitask ability that this involves. If avatars know a musician is playing to a real crowd, they like to attend and participate in the audience.

Crossover Marketing Strategies

Second Life® is a visually rich environment. Use it to your fullest advantage. Let your Internet, print, and television audiences know you're in Second Life®. Use photographs, links, machinima, and brand icons from Second Life® in your mass market material. You can generate fresh interest in your company, providing added support to the traditional strategies of reaching your target market. There's been enough press and Internet coverage on Second Life® that it's not completely foreign to the real world. As a matter of fact, it's fascinating and draws a lot of attention.

The Internet

It makes cyber sense for your virtual-world site to be supported by your traditional Web site. In fact, your Web site is an important part of your virtual-world presence. It provides event information, links, e-commerce, visuals, and contact information. You can include a link to your Web site in your personal and group profiles so that someone who is reading them has a place to go to learn more. We created Molaskeys-Pub.com to post stories, events, and pictures from Molaskey's in Second Life®. We also use the Web site for ad and sponsorship inquiries and to sell Pub shirts and sweatshirts.

Bring your virtual-world site to your Web site audience by providing SLurls, allowing them to teleport directly to your Second Life® location. If you are using other networks, such as Google groups, LinkedIn, Facebook, MySpace, Plurk, or any other online networking site, be sure to include your Second Life® association.

Television

If your company is already budgeting for television advertising, you can work your Second Life® presence into the script. Second Life® is making its way across the border to television. We've already seen it in prime-time television shows and featured on

Second Life® on TV

CBS created a dramatic episode of *CSI: NY* through The Electric Sheep Company that was focused on a Second Life® character. At the conclusion of the CBS airing of the Second Life® episode "Down the Rabbit Hole," the television audience was invited to log on to Second Life®, where they could explore a custom-built virtual world, specific to the *CSI: NY* program. Giff Constable of The Electric Sheep Company noted that they were prepared with four hundred sims to explore, which accommodated the burst of newcomers after the announcement.

Clear Ink also did some Second Life® work for television. NBC called on the company to produce machinima, the virtual-world equivalent of cinematography, for the prime-time comedy hit, *The Office*. Clear Ink produced a comedy skit, retaining a very SL-Realistic quality. Steve Nelson of Clear Ink noted that there was a viewer response survey of brand awareness. As it turns out, that Second Life® episode of *The Office* was very effective. According to IAG Research, it was one of the top ten most effective brand placements on TV last year. It was the only one not on a reality show and the only one not paid for by the brand. Second Life® ranked eight out of the ten most recognizable brands. That's remarkable.

the news and on news magazine shows, like *CBS Sunday Morning*. I predict Second Life®'s popularity to soar, and it won't be long before we see more television commercials filmed in Second Life® or even The Second Life® Channel.

Television tends to thrive on pop culture, and Second Life® is certainly a hot topic. Television producers are always interested in the latest trends. If you have an attractive or popular Second Life® site, make it available to television and machinima producers for filming on location in exchange for a crossover marketing strategy, where your site is given a name credit for the production.

Print

Making your Second Life® presence known through print is happening more and more. Just as we saw e-mail addresses appearing on business cards in the 1990s, we are now seeing Second Life® avatar names showing up on business cards today.

Magazines and newspapers are increasingly featuring the many facets of Second Life® as news stories. The color-rich pictures are appealing, and the stories and testimonies are even more fascinating. In a way, the print media are doing the advertising for you. Using the traditional print methods of marketing your Second Life® business may not be necessary, but if you already advertise your business that way, be sure to give a mention that you are now accessible through the virtual world of Second Life®.

Key Second Life® Marketing Tools

To support your efforts, you need to take advantage of some important marketing tools.

Classified Ads

Using the classified ads in Second Life® helps promote your product and services in-world. Though these ads boost your virtual-world presence, they should not be the only method of getting the word out about your products and services. Finding creative ways to promote your Second Life® business in the real world is strongly encouraged.

Placing a classified ad in Second Life® is as easy as filling in the blanks. When you open the search engine (found at the bottom of your screen, named Search), you have the option of searching things listed in the classifieds. When you open that section, you have the option of placing a classified ad. Simply fill in the blanks as prompted and offer a donation. The minimum donation is L$50 and can be arranged for weekly renewal. The more you pay for your ad, the better your chances are of being listed first in search results.

The classified ads you place show in the Classified section of your profile as well as in the Second Life® search. You can modify your ad through your profile as many times as you wish.

Search Results

Just as using certain keywords on the Internet gives you better search results, the Second Life® search engine works in a similar way. Use the main words describing the nature of your business, the items for sale, your services, and the business location. For instance, we use succinct words for searching Molaskey's Pub, such as "live music," "games," "parties," "pub," "Irish," "American," "culture," "friends," "events," "photos," "shops," "chess," "backgammon," and the like. Be sure not to use characters such as apostrophes or asterisks in your keywords, because they are harder for the search engine to identify.

Press Releases

The opening of your business in the virtual world of Second Life® may be newsworthy. If you have an established real-world business that is opening up a virtual-world office, consider submitting a press release to newspapers, magazines, radio stations, and cable and television networks. Get the word out. Even if your business is a small Second Life® start-up, with an interesting twist on the market, the real-world public will be curious to know how you're using the developing virtual world.

It is always advantageous to stoke a good relationship with the media and public. Second Life® is a community that thrives on communication and participation. Businesses that are joining the community may find they are welcomed with opened arms when they tend to some basic public relations.

Writing a press release can be a simple way of reaching the media to generate publicity. Make sure you use the correct format and wording. Consider whether the category of your press release would be considered news, product release, or social event. Members of the press will sort your announcement this way.

The press release follows a basic one-page format:

- a catchy headline and a dateline, which is the date and place of the event

- a paragraph of who, what, when, where, and why

- the body, which can be two or three short paragraphs, to offer the facts and details

- the boilerplate, which provides information on the person and company submitting the press release and their relevance to the subject

- the close of the press release, as indicated by the symbol ###, the word "End," or the number "30," and located under the boilerplate in the center of the page

- the contact information for the person receiving media inquiries, who may or may not be the same as the person submitting the press release

Submit your press release to news agencies and public relation firms. If you have the time and resources, you can find the media contacts on your own, but ensuring quick distribution and coverage to the right audience may be better left to the professionals. (There will be fees associated with submitting a press release through professional agencies.) On the other hand, if you are the one making the contact with the media, you have an opportunity to establish a relationship with them.

Video News Release

A video news release (VNR) is another way of announcing your arrival to the world. Second Life® is a visually rich world with the ability to record, edit, and play back like a video camera. You can create a machinima, or a video clip, about your business, product, or service. Marketing your business using visuals and a scripted storyline is an extremely effective way of getting noticed. With the ease and availability of video distribution sites, such as YouTube, you can post your VNR to the Internet, providing a link to and from your Web site. Major companies, government agencies, and small companies alike successfully and frequently use VNRs to announce products and services available to the market.

Virtual-World Giveaways

In the real world, companies often provide small trinkets and supplies to customers and potential customers in hopes of making a lasting impression. These goodies have a company logo on them, as a reminder to a customer of the company or product. These marketing giveaways are usually mouse pads, notepads, mint tins, mugs, or t-shirts, which people use or wear after the event, and marketing budgets have to account for these giveaways, often saving them for the most impressionable events. In the virtual world, the same strategy is used, but the giveaways hardly break the marketing budget or wind up in landfills.

Items in the virtual world can be reproduced at no cost. One of the most common giveaways in the virtual world is a t-shirt. They are easy to make, and people like wearing different clothing on their avatars. Although t-shirts are an easy giveaway, most avatars wear them only once or twice before they feel like a walking advertisement for your company. Some companies really grasp the idea of the no-cost marketing giveaway and produce unique, virtual-world collector's items. Major League Baseball offers Yankees and Red Sox memorabilia in Second Life®, allowing people to carry the famous rivalry into the virtual world.

When I organized a Pub Crawl, inviting nine pub owners to collaborate on a marketing event, each pub owner was to create a giveaway item showing its logo for

Pub Crawling patrons during the three-hour event. Of the nine participating pubs, Prop Spinners Pub best embraced the opportunity to market its unique establishment. They provided a complete outfit, with functioning gears and steam pipe top hat, which was expertly made with the pub's signature industrial and Victorian-era style. I think this giveaway is cherished most by participants. Long after the event is over, I have seen people wearing their Prop Spinners outfit from the Pub Crawl.

Another popular marketing giveaway comes from the tourist sims, like Dublin, Scotland, London, and Australia. They provide giveaway items specific to their countries and cities, such as flags, costumes, hats, and other props. Just as in the real world, tourists proudly wear and carry items from the places they've been or feel closely associated with.

The best marketing giveaways seem to be the ones that are expertly crafted, relevant to an event or special place, and offered for a limited time. They should also be something that avatars proudly wear, becoming the envy of other avatars wanting cool gadgetry and costumes. Releasing marketing giveaways during special events stimulates interest in visiting your site.

Get Your Message Out!

By far, the best way to engage Second Life® avatars is through interaction. Becoming involved in creating and expanding the virtual world is not just about investing in a marketing platform. When you and your business become part of the Second Life® community, you quickly find that you are investing in innovation, creativity, and immersive experience. You are investing in a way of life, albeit a second one. You will receive more attention by contributing things like innovative architecture, immersive product demonstrations, and an enjoyable evening at a concert than by implementing traditional marketing methods.

So get involved. Make the most of the technology and really be a part of this thriving community. Then you can listen as your company becomes a Second Life® household name.

12.

Selling Your Products and Services

Using the virtual world to sell your products and services allows you to be innovative in the way you reach out to your customers. The 3D virtual world allows you to sell a product or service in a selling environment that engages, compels, and persuades buyers.

Selling Virtual Products

There are countless profit-generating businesses in the virtual world, and they cater to fashion, sim decor, fetishes, entertainment, and various makeovers that appeal to the vanity of avatars. Having created a virtual-world good, business owners can set a price, place it out on a sales floor, and use the marketing methods that work for them.

The business owners I interviewed are making profits ranging from $50,000 to $300,000 selling virtual-world goods and services in Second Life®. Most of these successful business owners started with no money from the real world. They simply put their profits into growing the business. These savvy virtual-world business owners include a fashion retailer, a game maker, a real estate developer, architects, virtual-world business developers, and digital marketers, to name a few. They are able to make a profit in Second Life® because they all embraced the virtual-world medium. They all created attractive stores or offices and brands, and they invested their time and talents to build and market. Most important of all, they become involved with the community.

Volume Sales

Consider that you can produce a virtual-world product, such as a dress, and sell it for L$500 (approximately US$1.85). You might spend several hours creating this digital couture, and that time is certainly worth more than US$1.85. However, because there is no cost in reproducing the product, you make up your expense in time with sales volume. You might sell hundreds or even thousands of the dress over a few months, creating a profit well worth the time it took to produce an original.

Customers willingly pay an average of L$300 for digital couture. Virtual-world clothing does not require alterations or cleaning, so no further expense is involved. You can wear it over and over again, and it looks as fresh and new as the day you bought it. You certainly grow tired of it before it looses its wearability. Many people recycle their digital clothing, donating it to newbie friends or consignment. Sometimes they have a virtual yard sale to clear out their inventory, selling items at a discount from the original price. To determine the going market rate, do some research to figure out what people are willing to pay for your product, new or used.

Consistent and Gradient Price Structuring

Your pricing strategy should be consistent. Don't set your prices and then change them a few weeks later. Set your price with integrity, based on market assessment. Compare your product and services to similar ones already on the market. Include this market analysis and a summary of the competition's pricing in the pricing strategy section of your business plan.

If you are providing a unique product or service, perhaps a gradient pricing system will work for you. With such a structure, you begin with an incentive rate to attract new customers. Then, as your product and services improve, and as demand increases, you can justify a price increase. Make sure you reward loyal customers with special treatment in order to retain them through your price increase.

Creating a Sales Environment

Molaskey's Pub was selected by the virtual-world marketing company Millions of Us to participate in a virtual-world promotion for their client, Diageo, a worldwide liquor distributor for brands like Tanqueray, Guinness, Johnny Walker, and Captain Morgan. The company created and installed an interactive wall unit fully stocked with their brands. An avatar could order a virtual drink from the bar, which verified age prior to dispensing. Having received the virtual drink, the avatar was prompted to participate in a rowdy cheer or received comments, such as "Time for another Tanqueray!" This kind of product placement worked because it was in context with its environment and it interacted through chat. It became a Pub attraction.

Two keys to creating a product sales environment in Second Life® are

1. Pick your place.

2. Interact with the crowd.

For example, you wouldn't do a product promotion for grass seed at a winter festival; your product would be better placed at a garden show. The same applies in the virtual world. The liquor promotion wouldn't be as appropriately placed anywhere else. Choosing the location for the greatest impact is critical to your promotion. And having an interactive product demonstration gives you an edge.

Creating an Immersive Sales Presentation

When I met with Jon Brouchoud (SL Keystone Bouchard) on Architecture Island, he demonstrated how he uses 3D building for real-world applications. He simply dropped a sphere onto the land, and it unfolded before us as a structure. We walked around in conversation, pointing out the features of the building, its landscape, and color schemes. Within minutes of our tour, the structure disappeared, returning itself to inventory. Then Keystone dropped another building onto the ground, which unfolded before us, ready for a tour.

It was one of the best presentations I had ever experienced. And that's the point: I *experienced* it. This was not a PowerPoint or video presentation; it was an experience. If companies should consider Second Life® for any feature, it's the power of presentation. Imagine having the power to present your potential clients with real-time 3D sales demonstrations with style and character. Entire landscapes can be built, products and services can be demonstrated, and they can even be taken for a virtual test drive. Consultants can demonstrate processes, such as management plans and workflow.

The virtual world can be used to demonstrate any system in the same interactive manner that IBM uses for the healthcare system. The product in this case is a centralized and organized electronic health record that tens of millions of patients can securely manage and that authorized healthcare providers can access in emergency medical situations. At Virtual Healthcare Island, IBM is able to effec-

Selling a Brand

When extended into the virtual world, certain products and brands reach a market that identifies with and willingly interacts with their favorite brands. This kind of devotion carries over into the real world, where luxury items are much more accessible. Even if people aren't buying them in the real world today, they don't hesitate to get them in the virtual world, developing a relationship with the brand until one day they buy the real thing.

Several car companies, including Pontiac, BMW, and Toyota, have used the virtual world of Second Life® for product promotion. They are appealing to a market that is devoted to their brand, image, and lifestyle. These promotions are geared to the 20-something car enthusiasts and online gamers, a demographic that has grown up online. Selling a brand the virtual-world way makes a lasting impression on them. Although reality may keep them in a third generation hand-me-down car to get to school and an entry-level job, they're living it up while they're online. The vehicle promotions include garage-theme parties, sports cars on display, and virtual road testing the latest model and concept cars.

tively demonstrate how its system can save patients and providers from having to transfer records manually from doctor to doctor or from place to place. IBM is using Second Life® to deliver that idea by demonstrating the process in a simulated, interactive environment.

Using Second Life® as a 3D Diorama

Imagine you are bidding on a complex, real-world construction job. You can replicate the site in the virtual world and film the development, demonstrating the process of your bid from start to end. By using a storyboard filmed in Second Life®, you can effectively depict the stages of your plan and then bring your clients to the 3D site for

IBM's Virtual Healthcare Island

In February 2008, IBM launched the IBM Virtual Healthcare Island (http://www-03.ibm.com/press/us/en/pressrelease/23580.wss). Many IBM islands are used as sales tools to demonstrate a technology product. On Virtual Healthcare Island, IBM demonstrates how a total healthcare system using IBM technology can be efficiently managed, saving patients and healthcare providers time, money, and potentially lives. They are presenting the situation and the solution to the healthcare industry in a simplified step-by-step process.

The process begins with an avatar in a home environment, where she creates her electronic medical record (EMR) by entering information into a secure, universal electronic health record system created by IBM. The avatar can also set personalized health directives, such as authorizing a spouse or other immediate family members to make decisions about healthcare in the event that she is not able.

The avatar moves along to the next medical setting, the Virtual Healthcare Island Laboratory. The avatar demonstrates the real-world patient accessibility of the HIE system at each juncture of the medical journey. Next, the avatar/patient can visit the section of Virtual Healthcare Island known as the Clinic, where she meets with a primary care physician simulating a patient exam. They discuss the information from the electronic health record, including lab results and history. The physician updates the patient's chart, orders prescriptions, and updates the electronic health record with each visit.

Continuing the personal healthcare demonstration on Healthcare Island, the avatar arrives at the pharmacy to order prescriptions and receive drug information. By using the health information exchange (HIE) as demonstrated, consumers receive medications they presently require and are alerted about potential drug-to-drug interactions. They receive their verified prescriptions and updates on their personal, secure, electronic health record.

The hospital and emergency room on Virtual Healthcare Island simulate an emergency medical episode where a patient experiences the benefit of having a personal electronic medical record available to hospital and emergency staff to ensure proper treatment.

an up-close demonstration. The 3D element really adds the wow factor, getting your message across very effectively.

Because you can designate sections of your Second Life® island as public and private, your builders and designers can be busy at work on your 3D interactive diorama in total privacy. As they complete each region, invite your salespeople to become familiar with it. The salespeople can utilize the space as a showroom, hosting clients while giving a tour and literal demonstration of products, services, and abilities. Though you may choose to keep your sales area private, make sure you have a reception area open to all visitors. Equip your reception area with information boards and links for anyone to access, as well as some engaging features.

Immersive Second Life® sales presentations welcome your clients to participate in your sales presentation. Clients can then tell you what they see as potential strengths or concerns with your product or service, allowing you to respond in real time.

Prepare an Information Video of Your Presentation

Use the medium to its fullest extent. Hire a machinimatographer to record a Second Life® demonstration. Essentially, machinima is the virtual-world equivalent to video taping and editing a storyboard or demonstration. Most people can work a video camera, but to create a professional-grade video for business, I recommend hiring a professional. It is possible to record machinima from the tools found in your toolbar, but it is not a feature I use regularly. Torley Linden, Linden Lab's community instructor, has prepared a tutorial for anyone to learn how to use the machinima tools. The tutorial can be found online at http://wiki.secondlife.com/wiki/Video_Tutorials.

Post the completed video on your Web site as an information video or as a video news release (VNR). You can also send it along with a press release to the media and public relations professionals. Send customers an e-mail blast, announcing the availability of your 3D demonstration, attaching a link to the demonstration video. When they contact you, arrange to meet them in-world and impress them with a personal demonstration.

IBM's Virtual Healthcare Island was featured this way. They created a 3D diorama, created a storyboard to demonstrate the management process, and then filmed it as machinima in Second Life®. The completed video was released as a VNR and added to their information on their Web site.

Sales Strategies

Virtual-world business is not all profitable. Just as in the real world, not every business is a success. Unprofitability could be due to management practices, marketing skills, enthusiasm, lack of product demand, or even just timing and luck. But by paying attention to basic sales strategies, you can successfully navigate the ups and downs, ins and outs, of the marketplace.

Trends

In the real world, retailers rely on store planning, layout, theme, color schemes, product placement, and atmospheric music to prompt shoppers to buy. Simone Stern, a successful retailer in Second Life®, uses the same methods in her virtual-world shop. In addition, Simone can change her inventory much faster than in a retail store, so she is able to control her seasonal wear according to trends and customer demands, anticipating what they want before they even know what they want.

Pay attention to the avatars. What are they wearing? Where are they going? What are they doing? Spotting or even creating the next trend could be your key to success.

Sales and Freebies

As in the real world, the virtual-world businesspeople know that nothing gets the attention of the consumer better than the words "free" and "sale." If you feel you need something to boost your traffic and sales, have a promotion, like a three-day megasale, or offer a free pair of shoes with the purchase of a dress. Shopping incentives can be listed as an event in Second Life® Events, for free, through secondlife.com.

Virtual-world clothing retailers offer decent-quality clothing for newbies, who often start out with no money while they get their virtual-world bearings, for free or at drastically discounted prices. Getting newbies into the stores for free items allows them to see what's available for sale when they can afford to buy more. Having freebies to offer generates traffic.

The more traffic you generate on your site, the better your chances are of landing on the first page of Second Life® search results, which generates more traffic, which leads to sales. People are more likely to shop at the busy places because if everyone's going there, they must be good. It's a consumer mentality that carries over to the virtual world.

Classified Ads

As already explained, using the classified ads through the Second Life® search engine is a good way of getting the word out to people who are actively looking to shop. List the items you have for sale, using smart keywords, to attract shoppers to your store. Use good snapshots of the items you have for sale, and set reasonable prices as an added incentive to buy.

Xstreet SL, the shopping Web site for the virtual world, is also a good place to list your items for sale. The site features hundreds of unique items, properly categorized and organized in a way that makes hard-to-find items easy to find. Refer to the site for any fees associated with selling your products through the service. Some vendors don't have a store in Second Life®, relying mainly on sales through Xstreet SL.

Service Fees

The virtual world presents business opportunities for almost anyone. You don't need to be a professional graphic art designer in real life to develop virtual-world skills. Professionals certainly have an advantage, but amateurs can develop skills well enough to get virtual-world work. Amateur rates are significantly lower than professionals', but using amateurs is a consideration when comparing the needs of a project and the fair market rate.

Professional services, such as building, are commonly compensated in Linden dollars upward of L$50,000–L$100,000, depending on the agreement. L$50,000 comes out to about US$185.00, which breaks down to about $23 an hour for eight hours of work. For quality, professional 3-D building, this is a fair market rate.

For high-level design and construction, which may include a business development plan, the fair market rate reaches US$100 an hour or more, depending on your specific virtual-world goals and time frame. Full-service virtual-world companies of this caliber include The Electric Sheep Company and The V_3 Group.

Here is Apple MacKay's personal pricing rule:

> Pick two of the three following options: good, fast, or cheap. If you want something good and cheap, it won't be fast. If you want it fast and cheap, it may suffer on detail and quality. Fast and good will not come cheap.

Virtual-World Selling Do's and Don'ts

Do:

- Have a virtual-world promotion for your real-world product in an appropriate location or within a community that is in context with the product.

- Create a programmable script for your virtual product, whenever possible, which engages conversation and employs to the fun factor.

- Set your virtual-world product prices accordingly. Become familiar with the exchange rate and what people are willing to pay for products in the virtual world.

- Use Web sites like Xstreet SL, which specializes in selling virtual-world products.

- Create an interactive 3D sales presentation using Second Life®. Invite clients to *experience* your presentation.

- Keep up with seasonal sales adjustments, which ebb and flow as in the real world.

- Have a sale and offer freebies to generate more traffic to your site.

Don't:

- Be greedy by setting your prices too high. In the same sense, don't underprice quality goods.

- Overlook the opportunities to promote your virtual-world product in the real world and your real-world product in the virtual world.

Using a multidimensional interactive virtual world to cast a wider net may foster new methods of marketing, selling, and interacting with your customers. It is certainly providing new opportunities for entrepreneurs. There are multiple ways to use the virtual world for developing new products specifically for the virtual world, for marketing real-world products and brands, and even for bringing a virtual-world presence into the real world.

13.
Networking

A Web page offers two-dimensional communication: length and height. Visitors can only scroll around a page, going from link to link. The third dimension is depth of field. Depth is created in a simulator, where you can maneuver your view 360 degrees. In the third dimension, you are represented in a digital form—as an avatar—with the ability to digitally interact with people and objects around you.

There is, however, a fourth dimension: social connections. According to Grady Booch, "When we connect with others, we are exchanging intellectual and social compatibility. The fourth dimension introduces the human factor." The fourth dimension is also human personality, which comes through easily when others interact with your custom-made avatar. You create a look, but you also exude your intelligence and personal style through spoken language, chat, and gestures.

Interacting with others in Second Life® often yields valuable new connections. You are introduced to some interesting, knowledgeable people in Second Life® whom you might not otherwise meet.

Choose the Events to Attend

So many events, so little time. With the amount of events available to attend, you may be left scratching your head at the choices. Perusing event listings is a good way of finding free classes, discussion groups, bargains, parties, or live music events. Choosing what to do first may leave you wishing your avatar had a clone! By attending events that meet your interests, you give yourself the opportunity to mingle with the people who most closely represent your peers and possible business associates.

Each event draws people with similar interests. Attending a lecture on global warming will likely put you in the company of environmental activists, whereas attending a class on Second Life® basic skills will put you in the company of people new to Second Life®. You can surround yourself with people sharing your interests, or you can expand your horizons and try something new simply by attending one of the many organized events.

How to Find the Events That Interest You

Events are posted in the community section of the secondlife.com site, or, when you're logged in, you can use the search engine choosing the Events tab. The events are categorized as

- Discussion.

- Sports.

- Live Music.

- Commercial.

- Night Life/Entertainment.

- Games/Contests.

- Pageants.

- Education.

- Arts and Culture.

- Charity/Support Groups.

- Miscellaneous.

- All.

Each event is posted to the site by the event organizer and can be further categorized as Mature, for risqué or sensitive topics.

Another way to learn of events is by word of mouth. You can learn a lot by talking with others in the community and even peeking at their profiles. The people you meet may belong to groups of interest that you were not aware of, prompting you to investigate and explore.

If you belong to groups (and most people do), they will likely send you notices of their events if, and when, they have them. Not all group events are posted in the Event tab listing. You must belong to a group to receive their notices. Group notices arrive as a drop-down notice on your screen and often accompany a link directly to the location. When you are not online, the notice is sent to your e-mail. That service can be useful because you may receive an event notice that you are genuinely interested in attending. Receiving notices in your e-mail while you're not in Second Life® allows you to plan your schedule so that you can log on and attend during the set time of the event.

Groups Worth Checking Out

Here are some worthwhile groups you may consider joining based on a few general interests:

- *Metanomics*—about 1,100 members, founded by Prof. Robert Bloomfield of Cornell University. This group focuses on topics of business in the developing Metaverse. They host weekly lectures and several cutting-edge seminars. It is very active, with some of the most respected names in Second Life® as members.

- *NMC Guests*—over 4,000 members, founded by Larry Pixel. This group was spawned from The New Media Consortium, a highly respected group that includes universities, scientists, nonprofit organizations, philanthropists, and museums around the world. The Consortium invites NMC Guests to explore their campus and attend lectures, seminars, and exhibits in the areas of science, art, and education.

- *Live Music Enthusiasts*—over 3,000 members, founded by Astrin Few. This group was formed to alert members of live music performances ten minutes (or so) before show time. Joining is highly recommended for musicians, venue owners, and fans of live music. This group communicates mostly through group chat and can draw several people to a show, boosting traffic. One downfall is that the group chat is nearly constant, though relevant to the group mission; it pops up on your screen quite often. If that disturbs you, this group may not be for you. If that's the case, find a few musicians you like to follow and join their groups to be notified specifically of their performances.

- *SL Shakespeare Company*—about 1,400 members, founded by Ina Centaur. This is a professional theater troupe using Second Life® for high-quality live performances. They have one of the most visually rich environments I have seen in all of Second Life®. They offer events of a theatrical nature.

- *Real Life Education in Second Life®*—about 3,250 members, founded by Pathfinder Linden. This is a Linden Lab–sponsored group formed for the educators of Second Life® to network, collaborate, and share their experiences and education goals.

- *Macintosh Users*—about 2,600 members, founded by Phoenix Linden. Phoenix is an expert Mac user at Linden Lab. This is a support group for those—you guessed it—who use Macintosh computers. Members just type in a question, and several other members respond with answers.

- *Molaskey's Pub*—about 600 members, founded by Katydid Something. I can't pass up the opportunity to plug our group. We regularly feature live music and a friendly crowd.

Your Profile Is Your Resume

Your personality may speak volumes for you, but your profile is the book cover. Every resident of Second Life® has a profile, and most can be found through the search engine. When you open a profile, you are given several pages in which to get familiar with that person.

Your profile is akin to a social networking resume. It provides your virtual-world name, the date you entered the virtual world, your groups and affiliations, your Web site, your interests, and a few personalized words. Anyone can look at your profile at anytime without your knowing.

How to Make Sure You Come Across in the Best Light

The Second Life® profile is certainly more personable than a standard business resume. It contains a picture, partner information, favorite places, and a mention of skills and languages, which may humorously include typonese. Business resumes containing this information in the real world are typically eliminated from job consideration. In Second Life®, the more you complete your profile, the more information you are offering relevant to your Second Life® style, interests, skills, and experiences.

To create an impressive profile that reflects your personality and professionalism, start with the feature that gets noticed first: the picture of your avatar. This portrait can be anything you choose, but if you are in Second Life® as a real-life professional, consider using a basic headshot.

The next most noticeable part of your profile is the section listing the groups you belong to. As already mentioned, you are allowed to belong to up to 25 groups. The ones you choose give those looking at your profile some insight into your character. Some groups may make you seem business-minded, such as Metanomics, or as being part of a subculture with risqué fetishes. The groups in your profile make a statement about the time you spend in Second Life®. If you're there for professional networking, carefully consider your associations.

You are provided a section, under Groups, for free-form writing up to 500 characters. Use this section to state what you are doing in Second Life®, such as "I am a Human Resource Specialist with a major staffing company in New York. I am exploring Second Life® to consider the possibilities of opening a virtual-world office." After reading enough profiles of other people in Second Life®, you'll get the idea of the verbiage that best suits you.

On the second page of your profile, you are able to load the URL to your Web site. This is a live connection to your site, allowing people to click on it from your profile. It is a bit cumbersome, exploring a Web site from a small profile window, but, by offering it, you are providing reference to other areas of your life online. Viewers can always open their Internet browser to have a better look. If you have a Web site or a blog, I highly recommend including it in your profile, as long as it is relevant to you, just as if it were listed on your resume.

Assessing Other People's Profiles

Just as you prepare your profile for viewing, you can view others' profiles to assess their character. Do their pictures impress you? Are they partnered with anyone? What groups do they belong to? Do they seem like virtual-world Romeos or respectable community members? Do they use slang in their statements? Do they seem friendly or unapproachable? Do they have Web sites? What are their favorite places in Second Life®? Are their profiles complete, or do they seem incomplete?

The answers to these questions are determined by reading individual profiles, and they are the kinds of questions others will be asking themselves about you.

Just as a reminder, on the last page of a profile, there is a section called Note. This useful feature allows you to keep a cheat sheet about persons you meet and want to remember. Making a note in this section of a person's profile helps you recall their connection to you. Although it is kept in another person's profile, the Note section is a note to yourself, for only you to see. You're going to network with countless people in Second Life®. If you're anything like most of us, you'll likely forget the date, the place, or how you know someone. When you meet them again, or when they clearly remember you, you can quickly reference your notes.

Technicalities of Networking

This high-tech world, with its multiple dimensions and simultaneous conversations, is understandably intimidating to anyone seeing it for the first time. I felt the same way when I was an observer over Jay's shoulder. I was never one to play video games or chat online, but once I created my avatar and took a few (OK, many) tips from Jay, I just jumped in and tried my hand at it. I learned as I went, unafraid of being embarrassed or of asking many questions. Then I got pretty good at it. I still can't build a 3D object, but I can multitask and network in the virtual world, carrying on many conversations at once. When you figure out how to make it work to your advantage, using technology, no matter how advanced it seems at first, becomes less and less intimidating when you use it enough, and eventually it becomes rote.

Type-chat

The basic form of communication is type-chat. Whatever you type in the chat line can be read by avatars within a 20-meter diameter, which is public chat. If you need to be heard beyond the 20-meter range, type in the chat line, touch Shout (located at the end of the chat box), and then hit Enter, thus doubling your chat range. Use the shout feature only as needed. Shout-talking in general is rude.

Instant Messaging

If you want to have a private conversation with someone, use the instant message (IM) feature. You can access this feature by opening an avatar's profile and hitting the Instant Message option. This instantly opens a private chat line to the person. Anyone may do the same with you. You will know you're in a private chat with someone when it comes up on your screen with an "IM:" preceding the message. A new tab pops up above the chat line indicating you have received an instant message. To respond in IM, open the Instant Message tab, which opens a communication window. Click on the tab with the messager's name, and type your response in the instant message chat line.

You may be at an event or in a forum full of people and want to contact someone for a comment he or she made. If you're comfortable using the Instant Message feature, you can discretely introduce yourself and make your comment or ask a question without involving everyone within earshot. Take the opportunity to start a conversation with someone this way. Most people respond to an IM, appreciative of your interest.

Group Chat

Another way of conducting an instant message is with group chat. Members of a group can conduct a type-chat conversation just as individuals can. The difference is that this kind of chat is open to the entire group. Some groups have just a few close-knit members, whereas other group chat reaches thousands of members instantly.

Voice Chat

Voice-enabled residents—that is, those with USB headphones connected to their computers—have the option of speaking with individuals or groups. There is no additional charge for using the voice feature, making it especially enticing. You can speak through Second Life® to someone located on the other side of the globe for as long as you want at no charge.

When to Give Out Personal Information

People in Second Life® tend to guard their real-life information very closely. For a great number of people, Second Life® is an alternate life, which they prefer to keep separate from their real life. For others, it is an extension of their real life.

I know someone in Second Life® who is a powerful executive with a big company on Wall Street. While in Second Life®, he leaves his executive position far behind and enjoys the virtual world for its entertainment value. For him, Second Life® is an outlet not to be meshed with real-world responsibilities. He's in Second Life® not to network or to start a business, but for the social aspects. There's no reason for him to give out personal information. It's not relevant to what he's there for. I know what I know of him because I had the pleasure of meeting him in real life. Yet even in real life, he went by his Second Life® name, not his real name. His identity—what I minimally know of him—is safe with me.

You'll know when to give out your personal information, such as your real name, geographic location, profession, and contact information, depending on how you are using Second Life®. If you are there solely for the socializing, keeping your activities completely separate from your real-world profession, you may be more comfortable keeping your information private. If you are there to give your already public career a boost and to network for business, then make your information available because doing so is relevant to your goals.

Shed Your Newbie Status and Put Your Ideas into Action!

If you are able to navigate around Second Life®, to work with the communication tools, to use the search function, to create and join groups, to offer and accept friendship, and to change your outfit and accessories at will with style and flair, congratulations! You're no longer a newbie. You've achieved social status in the virtual world by fine-tuning your skills and participating in the community. You're "on the scene" and building a reputation. You're becoming known in certain circles and making your mark on the world. You've joined the ranks of the millions of enthusiastic residents of Second Life®.

When you join groups, attend events, and make contacts, you are establishing a presence in a world that is technically virtual but that is actually very real. The avatars represent real people, each with a diverse set of skills and resources. Using the technology of the virtual world, you have successfully connected with people based on specific interests in a shared environment.

Now that you understand what Second Life® is, learned a few technical skills, personalized your avatar, polished up your profile, and joined a few notable groups, being in-world is getting to be more and more comfortable. Chatting with others and participating in events are even becoming enjoyable. Now it's time to take it up a notch.

When you joined Second Life®, you may have decided to take an open-ended let's-see-what-happens approach. As long as it wasn't costing you anything, you were willing to see what all the excitement is about. If you've come this far, you likely can attest to how networking can happen so naturally in this environment.

You're meeting dozens of new people, enthused by the same spark of inspiration to expand their horizons as you are. Ideas on how to start or improve your business become part of a regular discussion. Don't let these valuable discussions go to waste. Act on them!

When we first began exploring Second Life®, and bought the land in Wichi, we hadn't fully developed a plan. Even when our new friends, Katydid and Gilly, joined the neighborhood, the idea to develop a business together was not fully realized. We just knew that we were on to something, and we experimented with the ideas we came up with. When Apple was approached to build a pub for a sim developer, he bid on it at a very reasonable rate. When they balked at the price and hired a less experienced builder at less than half the rate, Apple challenged himself to build a pub within the same tight deadline as the sim developer gave him. Without hesitation, Katydid offered her land, and Molaskey's Pub was created. By acting on an idea at the time of inspiration, our virtual fate was sealed. Molaskey's Pub was ready for business, opening on St. Patrick's Day, 2007. When you have an idea and act on it, you may be surprised at the results!

Expanding Your Network

Reaching your goals may require you to go back to the contacts you made during your planning stages. So keep track of the people you meet along the way. Maintain your relations and stay on good terms with all people. Many of the contacts we made when we started using Second Life® are still reliable resources for a variety of reasons. It's nice to see how far our contacts have come, acting on their ideas long ago. Over time, the contacts you make become more meaningful, having developed a history together.

Having a new set of contacts through Second Life®, brimming with innovative ideas and interesting collaborative projects, you may be enticed into playing a larger role with some of your groups. Although you may be busy developing your business and putting your entrepreneurial ideas into action, you should continue to develop relationships with the groups you joined and the people you met along the way.

Consider being a regular attendee of the events and become acquainted with more members.

When you attend events, contribute to the conversations, and make connections, you are continually expanding your reach. Each person you meet and add to your network may have something unique and valuable to contribute to your experiences. Your contacts are an infinite and evolving network, and you are part of it. Perhaps what you have to offer the world enriches the lives of others.

Demonstrate your real-world leadership skills by becoming a project manager for a group. Although you will likely do this on a volunteer basis, you will receive public praise for your work.

Don't limit your network to just Second Life®. Expand your network to include several other social networking sites. Let the social networking world know of your association with Second Life® and vice versa. If you belong to other groups and associations, check to see whether they are already in Second Life®. If not, why not recruit them?

When you reach out to the world, very often someone is reaching out to you at the same time. When you meet people with whom you share an interest, whose work you respect, or simply whose personality you enjoy, extend the hand of friendship. When you do, make notes about when and where you meet someone, also noting whether you were referred to her or she was referred to you and by whom. These notations come in handy because you will create a lengthy list of friends and acquaintances. It helps to know, after some time has passed, where you left off your last conversation.

You will call on your friends for various reasons, such as when managing projects or organizing events. Having a lengthy friends list becomes a valuable resource when you need questions answered, and you have people on hand with those answers. It also helps to have friends with certain skill sets. You may find yourself introducing people on your friends list, recognizing they may help each other, and they will credit you for the connection. It's all about making connections and maintaining them.

When you create a group, enrolling people may take some time. Molaskey's is a popular place that has been recruiting members since March 2007, currently with about 600 members. That's a respectable size for a group, though it pales in comparison to some others, like Metanomics or Live Music Enthusiasts. The difference is that Molaskey's is a social group, managed on a part-time basis. The larger groups are maintained daily, nearly around the clock, having a mission that requires that kind of effort.

When using your groups—whether large, medium, or small—to produce interesting social and business events and ultimately networking opportunities, you are creating the type of group that people want to join. As Grady Booch mentioned, networking is the optimal way to use Second Life®. People who have been in Second Life® a while are very particular about the groups they join. If you offer them a group that provides them with opportunities to have fun, effectively network, and make valuable connections, your chances of recruiting members are greatly increased.

Mia Kitchensink, Molaskey's Pub host, has singlehandedly recruited hundreds of members to our group. Whenever we have an event, she is there, getting to know almost everyone who comes to the Pub. If she has not seen someone around the Pub before, she personally extends a group invitation. This is an extremely effective method for us. We also offer a click-to-join option for those passing through in the off hours, when no one is around. Establishing your group with open enrollment is also very inviting.

14.
Meetings

Companies are always seeking inventive ways of cutting costs without cutting the quality of their product or service. One of the first things under scrutiny is the cost of travel. As a former business travel coordinator, I know that an average two- or three-day business trip, involving car service to the airport, an airline ticket, a car rental, a hotel stay, and meals, can cost thousands of dollars per person, not to mention the time lost in getting from one place to another. Although certain business trips remain an absolute necessity, gone are the days of traveling on a whim. Grady Booch, a seasoned business traveler for IBM, claims that Second Life® is an "economically viable substitute for travel."

I was able to meet with Grady in Second Life® only because he was traveling for business, as he often does. We could have just held a conference call, but instead we met through our avatars, adding the human dimension to the interview, and spoke to each other using a headset. He logged in from a satellite office, while the IBM moderator was in the corporate office, and I was at my desk at home. I was wearing a t-shirt and lounge pants, keeping it comfortable in real life while my avatar wore a suit. Using a USB headset, which enabled voice interaction through the computer, we sat our avatars in a public courtyard at the foot of IBM's famed Labyrinth and spoke for an hour. The meeting was as easy as any phone conversation, but in addition to conversing we had the sense of presence.

Grady noted that he meets with people all over the world using Second Life® while he is in real-world transit. He explained, "It enables you to multitask like never before because you are eliminating time-constraining travel while accomplishing a great deal."

Virtual-world meetings are quickly reducing and for many even replacing business travel. When you can arrange meetings and seminars accommodating two to two hundred people at a fraction of the cost by using the virtual world, cost-conscious companies are going to embrace this money-saving alternative.

Dr. Larry Johnson of The New Media Consortium, a leader in virtual-world development for art, culture, and education, organizes several large conferences a year. What used to be a time-consuming, expensive meeting, involving travel, catering, room rentals, and other arrangements, is now an efficient, productive gathering of professionals because it is done entirely in the virtual world.

Checklist to Prepare for a Meeting in Second Life®

Organizing a meeting in the virtual world requires the same preparation as a virtual-world event, with the added element of coordinating real-world attendees who are accustomed to real-world meetings. Perhaps you should start with a few small-scale meetings before having a company-wide or executive board meeting in the virtual world. Once you get through the first few virtual-world meetings, you can fine-tune the process, eliminating the bugs.

- Check the sim for lag and optimal performance. Identify what, if anything, is causing lag, and correct or remove it.

- Sometimes, Linden Lab brings the simulator down for maintenance. Make sure the sim is not scheduled for maintenance during your meeting by contacting Linden Lab concierge services.

- Create an environment that is conducive to your business meeting, such as a center stage amphitheater with the company logo strategically placed.

- Create an agenda for the meeting and place it near the stage, the focus of attention.

- Install and test audio and visual streams and video screens.

- Decide where and when to have attendees land. Allow enough time, perhaps 15 to 30 minutes prior to the scheduled meeting, for a meet-and-greet, as well as for attendees to arrive and get settled.

- For large meetings, coordinate a few landing spots, evenly distributed among attendees so that they don't land all at once on the same spot. Create and test a SLurl for those spots.

- Notify attendees of the scheduled meeting and their expected arrival time by e-mail, with a SLurl to the designated landing spot.

- Have attendees create their avatar well before the meeting. Offer a pre-meeting orientation, if necessary.

- Attendees should RSVP the meeting with their real names and their avatar names.

- Have clear signage at the landing spot and one or more persons to greet and direct arriving attendees to the meeting manager for check-in.

- Provide ample seating, and instruct attendees to take their seats as soon as they arrive. They will be able to adjust their view of the center stage without moving their avatar around. Staying in their seats reduces crowd congestion and the risk of avatar crash.

Use of Group Chat at the Meeting

Although the voice of your main speaker, moderator, or panel will reach the entire region of your meeting, the room chat between attendees will reach only a 20-meter range. Invite those with commentary to use group chat. As long as everyone at the meeting is in the group, which you may create specifically for the meeting, all attendees can read and contribute their comments no matter where they are sitting. Moderators can select questions from the group chat for the speakers to answer using voice.

Streaming Preferences at the Meeting

Advise attendees to set their Streaming Preferences as follows:

- Go to Edit at the top of the screen.

- Touch Preferences located at the bottom of the Edit drop-down menu.

- When the Preferences window opens, touch the Streaming Preferences tab.

- Set the preferences to Play Streaming Music Whenever Available and to Play Streaming Media Whenever Available.

Overcoming Technology's Little Interruptions

Crashes

One of the interruptions that can occur in a Second Life® meeting is the somewhat inevitable crashes—when a computer becomes overloaded and freezes. To remedy this condition, you may need to force-quit the Second Life® program and relog (i.e., log in again). If that doesn't work, you may need to restart the computer and rejoin the meeting. Luckily, one of the options when relogging is to return to your last position. You don't have to enter through the reception area or reenter the meeting. You just reappear where you last were, though in a standing position. Simply click to sit in your seat again and resume your role in the meeting. However, when you crash and relog, you may miss out on several valuable minutes of the meeting while you're gone.

Client Lag and Server Lag

There are two kinds of lag: client lag and server lag. Client lag is blamed on the user's computer, which may be unable to render the world at a decent frames-per-second (FPS) rate. Anything below 8 FPS is practically unusable. Older machines or machines with a low-performing video card will struggle. You can alleviate some of your lag by adjusting your preferences and heeding the advice given later in this section.

The other type of lag is server lag. The simulator, or server, that is maintained by Linden Lab may also generate lag. Optimally, that server should run at 45 FPS—and you can never have too many FPS—but it may be running more slowly than usual. Time dilation, or the reason that Second Life® can run in real time, can also create lag. Still another source of noticeable lag is the engine that cranks the physics part of the simulator. Linden Lab handles these technical issues, but you can access the statistics menu that displays the related readings by holding down either the Apple key+Shift+1 on a Mac or Ctrl+Shift+1 on a PC.

To reduce lag and the tendency to crash, you can optimize your computer's performance in several ways while logged on to Second Life®.

Sim Managers

- Checking the sim for lag and optimal performance is a technical task that should not be overlooked. Tech-savvy users with authorization to manage a sim know to look at the FPS rate by opening the statistics menu. You may be able to identify what is causing your lag and work with a Linden Lab specialist to fix the issue.

Everyone

- Adjust your system preferences by going to Edit at the top of your screen. Click Preferences at the bottom of the resulting drop-down menu, and that opens your Preferences window. Touch the Web tab and see Clear Now, which clears your browser cache. Then go to Graphics and set your Quality and Performance to Low. You can adjust these settings at another time, when you are not in a crowded sim.

- Close all other applications on your desktop that are not in use.

- Keep your camera movement to a minimum when on a crowded sim. If you draw back for a wide-angle view, your screen will fill up with more information to process, causing you to lag and possibly crash.

- Refrain from taking snapshots during crowded events.

- Detach scripted vanity items, such as face lights, flashy jewelry, and other accessories.

Privacy

Having meetings requires varying degrees of privacy. Privacy can be achieved in Second Life® by using the group chat Instant Message feature, thereby establishing a voice conference with an entire group or with specific people using a USB headset. Private land access, requiring visitors to be on an authorized list or arrive by personal invitation, is another way of achieving privacy in Second Life®.

Private Group

For large group meetings, you may consider creating a group by invitation only, not open to public enrollment. The private group can be created and maintained by a meeting manager specifically for private meetings. As people arrive during a scheduled meeting, they are greeted and directed to check in with the meeting manager, who verifies their names on the guest list and offers them an invitation to the temporary group. For the duration of the meeting, the attendees can engage in private chat through the created group. When the meeting is over, the members of the

Keeping It to Yourselves

While working with a production crew for The Electric Sheep Company, filming at various locations in Second Life®, we used the private voice feature of a group created specifically for each production. As we were called onto the set, we activated the voice feature, then muted our microphones, so that the only people who were heard talking, in a group of about 12 people, were the director, producer, and production assistants. As an actress or an extra on a set, I was able to listen to the director, usually Martholomew Mip, and position or motion my avatar as directed for the shot. If I needed to speak, I unmuted the microphone on my USB headset, said what I needed to say, and muted myself again. That's not to say the rest of the cast didn't have continual group-chat while we were between takes! We carried on that way for hours.

Because we were on location in some public places, using the group voice feature was especially useful. I am certain it left many onlookers wondering what a group of avatars were doing standing around so silently! While we were chatting it up in group chat and group voice chat, no one outside the group was aware of our dialogue.

group, other than the meeting managers, are removed, leaving the group available to be used again. At the next meeting, meeting attendees are again invited to join the group. It's a form of group recycling for the purpose of privacy.

You can also use the private communication features, such as group chat or group voice, even if your group is scattered. What matters is not where people are, but what group they're in. For example, if you are taking a group on a guided tour of Second Life®, you can maintain a conversation within the group without receiving comments from passersby. The point is that you can have a private conversation with one or a thousand people at a time using the group voice feature by clicking the Join Call button in your group information. Members of the group can participate in the conversation if they have the voice-enabled features set through their preferences and a USB headset.

Private Land Settings

When you own land, you can establish privacy settings, preventing anyone to land on your property without clearance from you. However, this works only for land you are on. To adjust your land access permissions, you must be standing on your land; you cannot do this remotely.

To access the privacy settings:

- Go to World in the menu bar at the top of your screen, prompting the drop-down menu.

- Click About Land. The pop-up window features several tabs, one of which is Access.

- Check the box to allow public access, or leave it unchecked to activate the privacy setting.

You may grant access to your land by Group Affiliation or by Resident name. You may also sell access to your land. This feature may be activated and deactivated for special fund-raising events or live music concerts.

Parcels of land are set as public or private, with access granted to entire groups or to individuals, as directed by their owners. Island owners may choose to have a private island or a partially private island. They have total control over their property, designating certain areas or parcels of land for public and private use.

Skyboxes

In Second Life®, where we go beyond the laws of physics, inhabitable structures, called skyboxes, also exist in the sky. Because they're levitating high above the land, you can't just walk into and out of them. You have to be teleported. Although avatars have the ability to fly, most skyboxes are placed high above avatars' visual distance unless they really look for them. Even if a skybox is spotted, most of them don't have doors. They're literally boxes, kept plain on the outside and plastered with murals on the inside, creating a vast expansive illusion. They're cozy hideaways, far out of chat range and wandering explorers. For the most part, people forget they're there: out of sight, out of mind.

Skyboxes offer the most privacy. You can have a conversation in open room chat with very little chance of anyone eavesdropping. You can hold small, informal meetings in your skybox. We have Molaskey's Pub managers meetings in our hidden skybox. We have levitating seat cushions that form a circle. Although we may be actively speaking with one another, using the voice-enabled feature of Second Life® and real-world headsets, our avatars look as though they're peacefully meditating.

On and Off the Record—and the Radar Too!

Some say there is no privacy in Second Life®. That is a good point. Most of the communication that takes place in Second Life® is by way of typewritten chat, and any of this type of chat can be copied and pasted, even private chat. It is all on the record. If you wish to speak off the record, you have to go beyond private chat and into voice. Unless someone is using a recording device during a conversation, which is illegal without your consent, it is about as far off the record as you will get using Second Life®, unless, of course, you say nothing at all.

For conducting meetings, some prefer to use type-chat so that they have a transcript of the meeting. This can be very useful for obvious reasons. When the conversation goes too fast, you step away from the keyboard, or you miss a comment for whatever reason, you can simply go into chat history and get caught up.

A kind of radar device is also available. You can load a device onto your avatar that can detect other avatars within 96 meters (or so) of your position, indicating the names of all avatars and how close they are to you. This is for certain a useful gadget. It makes you wish you had one in real life. There're no sneak attacks or eavesdroppers with a gadget like that!

Meeting and Technology Services

Second Life® meetings can be as casual as a loose gathering of professionals in the Pub after hours or a formal departmental meeting in a space that accommodates well over 100 people. If you're not the type to design and build a high-tech meeting space in Second Life®, several professional services in Second Life® are poised to manage your occasional virtual-world meetings.

Here are some questions to answer when selecting a Second Life® meeting place:

- Is the meeting space located on the mainland or an island? A private island is preferred for large numbers of attendees.

- How many people can the space accommodate?

- Is the stage designed so that the attendees are all within chat range? If not, you need to consider creating a temporary group to include everyone in the chat.

- Are there breakout areas?

- Will a technical manager be on site during the meeting?

- Does the service include receptionists and a meeting manager?

- Will any other meetings or events be going on within a close proximity? Make sure the location is a comfortable distance from busy clubs and risqué shops. Even though a private space won't allow uninvited guests wandering about, their chat may spill into the meeting space. That could be a disaster for your business meeting.

- Will you have the ability to hang company logos and to stream videos and podcasts?

- How is the food? Just kidding! Catering is one less worry with a virtual-world meeting.

Search Second Life® using appropriate keywords to find a reputable SL meeting planner. You may also refer to the Second Life® Grid, the business services section of secondlife.com.

Linden Lab has an alliance with Rivers Run Red, a virtual-world business service provider. They are unveiling a service known as Immersive Work Spaces. They offer a program for online business meetings involving sharing and editing documents from desktop and downloading video presentations and podcasts with collaborators located anywhere in the world with the ease and access of using the Internet. The added value is that this special program utilizes the rich 3D environment and human element that Second Life® is known for.

More information about Second Life® business services and featured contractors can be found on secondlifegrid.net.

Navigating Time Differences

The virtual world of Second Life® runs on Second Life® time (SLT). Just as Linden dollars act as one currency despite what currency people around the world use, SLT is a unified time reference in Second Life®. When you arrange a meeting or an event in Second Life®, you refer to it in terms of SLT. For instance, concerts at the Pub take place every Sunday afternoon 12 P.M.–3 P.M. SLT.

The basis of this time reference is San Francisco, California, where Second Life® originated. For those in other parts of the world, the time difference can take some getting used to. For instance, events scheduled for Sunday afternoon means Monday morning in real time for parts of Asia and Polynesia.

When you arrange a meeting or event with people in various time zones, be sure to select an agreeable time that accommodates everyone. Although Molaskey's Pub is a measurable success in popularity, it operates in a time frame, which includes all U.S. and Canadian time zones, that enables us to manage it. We often have people arrive, looking for a crowd, but what may be considered prime time in some time zones is off time for us.

Always refer to time in Second Life® as A.M. or P.M., followed by SLT, so that people do not confuse their local time with virtual time.

Comparing Real-World and Virtual-World Meetings

Meeting packages vary in rates, depending on the level of service and the hours you book. Considering that outsourcing a real-world meeting could cost a company several hundreds if not thousands of dollars, using the virtual world seems like a bargain. Don't, however, mistake the bargain price as a compromise in service or results. You will be able to accomplish a successful corporate meeting for about 40 people in Second Life® for about L$55,000—about $200. For some real-world meetings, that would hardly cover the cost of lunch!

Let's make a quick comparison between real-world and virtual-world meetings:

- *Real-world* meetings may involve travel packages, catering, and time away from the home or office. The travel expense alone could run into the thousands.

Virtual-world meetings may involve teleporting and a home-cooked meal. Travel savings reaches into the thousands.

- *Real-world* meetings may require booking a conference room, which may or may not be available.

Virtual-world conference rooms are always available.

- *Real-world meetings* may require wearing a dry-cleaned suit; driving; flying; stopping for coffee and a breakfast sandwich; carrying equipment, cell phone, and briefcase; sitting in traffic; and worrying about being late. You do it all because you have a responsibility to your job and have to make a good impression. Life is stressful.

Virtual-world meetings reduce or eliminate the need for all that, ultimately reducing our carbon emissions, fast-food packaging, and waste. You sit comfortably in your favorite chair with a laptop or at your desk, wearing lounge pants and your favorite organic cotton Greenpeace shirt. The world is a happy place.

The main point is that when you choose to hold virtual-world meetings to collaborate with people located in different places, you are saving time, money, and effort without sacrificing the quality and content of the meeting. Also, you are making a green business decision. For all those reasons, you can make a positive impact on your employees, the Earth, and the all-important bottom line.

15.

Staffing the Metaverse

Whether you are hiring or looking for work, the virtual-world workforce is alive and well. No matter what the economy and job market of the real world are like, Second Life® has plentiful jobs and a thriving economy.

The start-up business owners of Second Life® often pay out of pocket for everything, including their staff, while launching their business. The microeconomy of Second Life® not only serves as a common global currency, simplifying the headaches associated with constantly exchanging real-world local currencies, it takes the sting out of running a business. Business owners typically pay hosts L$250–L$500 an hour, about US$1–2 an hour. Although the pay rates of Second Life® jobs are far below the minimum wage of a real-life job, many of the people working part-time jobs in Second Life® are happy to do so because they're being paid, even minimally, for their time online.

Most of the time, the money earned from these part-time jobs goes to sustain a resident's life online, not to pay their real-world bills. Rather than buying Linden dollars to support a Second Life® lifestyle, people work a few hours a week instead, gaining valuable experience and learning new skills while they do. And there are plenty of business owners who can use part-time help.

Interaction is an immensely important part of the successful virtual-world business equation. Your virtual-world site greatly benefits from having someone on a schedule to manage your site and to interact with visitors. It also takes the pressure off you or your real-world staff to constantly be there, wearing many hats.

You can consistently draw traffic to your site by having someone there to manage events when you're not online. Having someone available gradually increases your everyday traffic and business activity. When traffic is up, your business ranks higher in the search engine, generating more traffic and potential for sales. You can't possibly be there all the time, so consider hiring a trained avatar, familiar with the online environment, to be there when you're not.

A Variety of Jobs in Second Life®

You might not get rich with the part-time jobs in Second Life®, but you will be able to sustain your virtual-world lifestyle. Here are just some of the types of jobs typically found in Second Life®:

- *Hosts.* Almost every type of venue in Second Life® requires a host. Hosts simply need to be on location to greet arriving visitors, keep the conversation going, and answering visitors' questions. Some hosts are authorized to send group notices to draw people to an event. Hosts have to be personable and friendly.

- *Event managers.* An event manager works with venue owners in planning special events. They post events to the event listing, Web sites, and other avenues of publicity. They often are the ones to decorate, create signage, send notices, test landmarks, and greet arriving visitors.

- *Builders.* Although I have mentioned builders in terms of grand-scale developing, there are plenty of opportunities for builders to do the smaller jobs, too, such as for sims and landscapes. Not everyone has the skills to build in 3D, but being in a 3D environment presents many needs for that skill.

- *Designers.* Designers may work in the areas of fashion, landscape, architecture, or avatars or in any area that is made better by how something is built, functions, or looks. In a developing world, designers have many opportunities to employ their skills and to have them recognized.

- *Scripters.* Anyone with the skill and knowledge to animate 3D objects by programming them is in demand in the developing virtual world. Scripter rates vary on custom orders, but many items are available through their shops and can range from L$0 to several thousand Linden dollars per item.

- *DJs.* As a social network, Second Life® offers plenty of social events going on at any time, and most of these events require entertainment. DJs with the ability to stream media and work a virtual-world crowd are in demand. They use their own collection of music and play it in Second Life® through a broadband stream, like Nicecast, for instance. Not only does their taste in music determine their fit for a job, their personality does too. DJing in Second Life® is very much like hosting a small radio show. DJ rates vary, often ranging from L$250 to L$500 an hour, plus tips from appreciative fans.

- *Musicians.* Live music draws large crowds to venues because talented musicians have a devoted following. Just as a DJ streams music using a broadband stream, musicians wire their instruments to the stream and play live in Second Life®. Musicians are paid handsomely by venue owners, ranging from L$1,000 to L$10,000 an hour plus tips from the crowd.

- *Campers.* Some venue owners pay people to populate their venue so that they can maintain traffic. Campers don't have to interview for these jobs. They simply have to find a place offering the animation that automatically pays for the time you click it. The pay rate is usually about L$2 a minute with a maximum time allowed. It's easy money, but it's a mere pittance in pay.

- *Dancers.* Nightclubs and social halls sometimes hire people to animate their avatar to dance, making the club appear lively. Dancers also engage the crowd and encourage spirited conversation. Although "dance" can sometimes mean of the adult nature, it is not always the case; it depends on the club.

An Odd Job, Viewed by Millions!

I was getting paid L$8,000 to L$40,000 (remember that's in Lindens) for being a greeter, a mentor, and an extra in a film shoot, and for taking on all sorts of other odd jobs in Second Life®. I was able to build up a comfortable Second Life® income. From 2006 to 2007, my avatar, Nasus Dumart, was cast as an extra in several machinima works and big-name promotional events. Whenever a call goes out for a paying gig, it is always first-come/first-serve. They were hard to turn down because they were so interesting and paid well, in Linden dollars.

I once arrived for a typical machinima cattle call (as it was called). About five other odd jobbers and I were then offered a long-term gig doing several parts in machinima over several weeks. I knew it was a big project, but it didn't really matter what it was; I was just thrilled to be part of the project as an actor. SL™-Martholomew Mip was director, assisted by SL™-Danny Odell. The schedule worked for me, so I agreed to do it.

At the end of each workweek, I filled out a time card and submitted it to my designated manager. A week later, a deposit was made in my Second Life® account. It was very much a real job in terms of responsibility and pay. I even had to fill out tax forms before committing to the job pool, just as in a real-world job.

I was cast in multiple nonvocal roles in *CSI: NY* as Venus and White Rabbit, as well as just being an on-scene extra. Several of my big scenes made the cut to television. I controlled the costumed avatar from my keyboard at home through actions that were scripted by the talented production team. Neither the director nor the producers ever disclosed what project we were working on until we wrapped the shoot. The *CSI: NY* production I worked on was titled "Down The Rabbit Hole," featuring Second Life® for the first time on prime-time television (the episode originally aired on *CSI: NY* on October 24, 2007). I can proudly claim a place in Second Life®'s debut on television.

Second Life® Talent and Staffing Agencies

If you are looking for interesting temp work or have a position to fill, you have plenty to choose from in Second Life®. With so many businesses in need of a reliable staff for hosting and product demonstrating, many Second Life® residents are earning an income from home on a flexible schedule. Some staffing companies focus on specific areas of business, such as media, social events, or tech jobs.

The Metaverse Mod Squad, Second Life®'s hippest staffing agency, was formed in 2007 by Amy Pritchard (CEO), Michael Pinkerton (COO), and Peter E. Hilliard (president). It assembled a team of managers and staff and serviced some interesting clients in the virtual world, including Harry Potter, American Solutions featuring Newt Gingrich, Warner Brothers, and the CW Television Network.

The Metaverse Mod Squad finds their associates by recruiting tech-savvy people with experience in moderating traditional message boards. It also "finds some gems from the communities they work in." Many of their virtual-world staff are real-life stay-at-home moms, college and graduate students, disabled persons, or seniors who are thrilled to receive proper virtual-world training and work a few hours a day from the comfort of their own homes with a really fun group of people. A virtual-world job pool is a brilliant idea, which I think we are just seeing the beginning of.

Manpower Inc. is a global leader in employment services, with the motto, "You build the site, and we'll provide the avatars." The firm tapped into the new market of virtual-world staffing by establishing their Second Life® presence in 2007, calling it market research. The company soon recognized the potential in Second Life® and the virtual world's growing need for skilled, professionally minded people to work in it.

Semper International is another real-world staffing company that spawned a virtual-world annex. Semper recruits real-world graphic art professionals. After setting up an office in Second Life® to expand their reach with interactive media, its management decided to open a staffing company specifically for the virtual world. Virtual

Job Candy is a result of the many inquiries Semper received from employers and professionals about staffing the Metaverse.

The Electric Sheep Company created a group known as Odd Jobs, a job pool resource for the many part-time and contractual work they had available. In 2006 and 2007, Esheep, as they are affectionately called, grew in leaps and bounds, acquiring some of the biggest-name clients and exciting projects in all of Second Life®. Jobs were plentiful during that time. They recruited several people in Second Life® to work as greeters, hosts, actors, and extras on their client sites, such as *The NBA, Starfruit, AOL,* and several machinima projects. I had the good fortune to be part of that exciting time as one of the odd jobbers.

Getting a Job in Second Life®

Many jobs are posted in the search engine, organized by keywords, just like the classified ads in the newspaper. You can also place a classified ad, making it known to the world that you are in the market.

Networking in the circles that you want to work in is also a good way of getting noticed. Join the groups that you want to either work for or that will help you find work in Second Life® and beyond. Become a regular at their events and offer to take the lead on volunteer projects. Not all groups offer open enrollment. The ones that don't are usually reserved for serious participants. Introduce yourself once your profile and real-life resume are in order.

Is your college or university in Second Life®? If you have virtual-world skills, the school may be interested in hiring alumni for virtual-world projects. Perhaps it can also assist you with real-world job search efforts and interviewing methods. Many universities are represented in Second Life®. Check to see whether yours is there. If it does not have a campus, perhaps it is represented through the New Media Consortium or other education group. It may prove to be worth the time it takes to search.

Do:

- Have your resume or portfolio prepared for immediate viewing.

- Check the search engine for the companies, groups, and associations in Second Life® that you want to approach.

- Let it be known through your profile that you are interested in working in certain fields and have certain marketable skills. You will appear in the search results for the words you use.

- Introduce yourself to business owners. Most people in Second Life® are very approachable. Serious business owners appreciate skilled people approaching them, saving them searching time.

- Offer to volunteer on projects, gaining virtual-world experience and reputation.

Don't:

- Make a serious job inquiry without having a portfolio or your resume ready.

- Mistake virtual-world jobs as being less important than real-world jobs.

- Show up for an interview or meeting wearing wacky avatar accessories. Dress for the job you want, saving your playful side for the off hours.

Hiring in Second Life®

Just as applicants use the search engine to look for work, you can use it for finding applicants.

Do:

- Know what the market rate is for the job you need filled. Snoop around, and ask questions about the going market rate.

- Know how long you need a job to last.

- Establish a system for paying people, such as PayPal, Linden dollars, or any other method, perhaps a barter or trade.

- Provide an applicant with a specific job description.

- Provide a consistent schedule.

Don't:

- Delay paying the people who work for you.

- Switch the plan on someone who is counting on you for work. Fulfill your agreement with them.

Finding a Qualified Contractor

These are not the type of building contractors who have to brush the sawdust off their clothes and pull splinters from their hands. If anything, they are blowing bread-crumbs off their well-used keyboard (having many meals at the desk). Building contractors in Second Life® have a steady client base for custom building. They can also create prefabricated buildings to sell in a shop or through the classifieds.

You can use the Second Life® search engine to find just about anything, including people with the skills you need. When searching for a contractor, allow enough time to sift through the classifieds, groups, and people listed in the search engine using the keywords relevant to the job you need done. Most of the builders in

Second Life® work independently, but many others belong to consortium groups that job-share according to skills availability. This provides a one-stop shop for clients in need of several areas of development.

Many, many talented independent builders and scripters are available for work. As in the real world, go by their previous work, their referrals, and your instincts. If you find an independent contractor, ask to see his or her portfolio. Serious, established SL builders will have something to show you. Newly established contractors may not have a string of clients yet, but they may also be starting a new SL business and would be perhaps more eager to please you.

Depending on the size of the bid, you may need an agreement in writing. Many work arrangements made in Second Life® agree to payment in Lindens, though an alternate arrangement to pay the equivalent in real currency can be made. Payment exceeding US$600 in a year must be reported to the IRS, so keep good records, even if it *is* in Linden. Remember that Linden dollars add up to real U.S. currency. Check with your accountant if you are uncertain.

Some companies are well established in Second Life®, and their goal is to bring established real-life companies there. They are listed on the Second Life® Web site and usually have a package plan that includes their own builders, scripters, marketers, and other staff. Their fees may be relatively high, but they are very capable of getting the job done.

Recruitment for Real-World Jobs

Remember that your Second Life® profile is a resume. Real-world recruiters are active in Second Life®, and they're looking for the people behind the avatars, buildings, and businesses. The corporate world is making the transition to the virtual environment.

Recruiters are looking into Second Life®, learning about people and trends. They're using Second Life® for its superior networking ability, and they are keeping key people in mind when real-world positions open up.

Recruiters also hold job fairs in Second Life®, offering on-the-spot preliminary interviews. They then decide whether they will schedule real-world job interviews with the candidates they meet. If the interview is for an online job, a real-world interview may not be necessary. Even so, the virtual world's fourth dimension, which enables personality to come through, can support a person's qualifications for a job.

PART

5.

WHAT'S
TO COME

16.

The Evolving Metaverse

Philip Rosedale, the creator of Second Life®, abandoned the role of an almighty controller, preferring to develop enabling technology. He enjoys seeing the creative, expressive, and sometimes surprising ways people from around the world take advantage of the virtual world. Essentially, he built the vehicle and handed over the keys, putting the residents in the driver's seat.

Since 2003, there have been many drivers. The businesses that have either formed within Second Life® or moved into it have the advantage of saying they were among the early innovators. But in-world innovation is something that never ends. As you explore your role in Second Life®, remember that the only limit to imaginative building is the fact that no one has thought of it before.

Rosedale's vision of Second Life® is an example of that. His early enthusiasm for science fiction, physics, and technology became fused with a vision he had as a child of developing an entire world in cyberspace. By 1999, when he felt that the technology had caught up with his ideas, he began working on a virtual-world prototype. The technology had evolved to the point where a child's wildest dreams could come true. And the resulting virtual world is the vehicle for others to build on their ideas and dreams.

We have traveled beyond the Internet, its uses, functions, and refinements. We have introduced the 3D virtual-world platform and the ways in which to build an online presence using personality and imaginative, immersive structures. We have discussed the benefits of using the virtual world as an added feature to your Web site and for efficient meetings and networking. After having witnessed the technology, tools, and possibilities of 4D life online, you are probably asking, "What could possibly be next?" The answer is in the hands of technology and business experts planning the next stages. One of those experts is Zha Ewry, a Second Life® resident, the IBM architect working on open architecture, and someone we will have more to say about in the next section.

Preplanning the Roadwork of the Metaverse

Many virtual worlds make up the Metaverse, including massively multiplayer online games (MMOGs), massively multiplayer online learning games (MMOLGs), youth worlds, mixed reality worlds, private worlds, social networks, and many more. Each has a specific audience, and some people are involved in multiple virtual worlds to explore their various interests.

Currently, these virtual worlds run independently of one another. The term "metaverse" refers to virtual worlds collectively. As the leading architect on the IBM research team, Zha Ewry works closely with Zero Linden, of Linden Lab, experimenting with metaversal interoperability.

Just as the Internet needed to establish secure links to authorize the sharing of information, such as a credit card or social security number, virtual worlds need to establish secure links. Internet security is indicated with a secure sockets layer (SSL) certificate indicated by the prefix "https://" in the Web address. Ewry and members of the architect team are working on a way to securely teleport from one virtual world to another, a feature that requires a trusting relationship between worlds. To establish this trusting relationship with other virtual worlds, a preplanned secure system must be in place. This kind of progress, when ready for the world to use, will again change how we use the Internet and ultimately the Metaverse. Virtual worlds, evolving before our eyes, will have the ability to securely interoperate.

Achieving Interoperability in the Metaverse

Interoperability allows systems to work together, making for more useful and efficient performance. For systems to fully interoperate, universal standards, such as language (both technical and cultural), technical compatibility, and procedures, must be able to work flawlessly together. Interoperability requires a well thought-out plan promoting the convergence of several systems, departments, and policies for a greater purpose. Preplanning interoperability within the Metaverse at this early stage saves time, frustration, money, and egg on the face later.

The Hubble telescope is an example of what can happen when planning is not coordinated. The Hubble is a technical marvel created by astrophysicists and scientific explorers of the universe. Some of the smartest people on the planet built it, launched it into space, and waited with bated breath for images from the far reaches of the universe. When the first pictures returned, they were disappointingly blurry.

With a painstaking review of the details of the entire operation, the developers realized that the main mirror on the telescope had been cut to a different set of measurements than those specified for the rest of the telescope, putting the mirror out of synch and resulting in blurry images. It was one of the biggest oversights in modern scientific history. Engineers were able to correct the problem by creating a lens that fit over the mirror like a pair of glasses, eventually getting the stunning images they'd first hoped for. However, the corrective lens was costly in terms of money, time, and public confidence in the space program because the work had to be done twice. An old carpenter's mantra, recited by builders, is, "Measure twice. Cut once." This layman's rule serves as a reminder to use caution and to check measurements before any irrevocable cut is made.

The architects who laid the groundwork for the Internet are now collaborating on a grand-scale project for making the Metaverse interoperable. Having learned from the Internet's performance, how people use it, and its future potential, they are planning the big-picture function of a user-friendly, interoperable Metaverse.

Secure and efficient interoperability through the Metaverse will allow us to interact with more than one virtual world, giving users the ability to reach into the massive online world with extraordinary efficiency, for generations to come.

Linden Lab and IBM, working together to develop secure Metaverse travel, were able to successfully teleport a handful of avatars between Second Life® and a private world located securely behind IBM's firewall. It was the virtual-world equivalent of landing a man on the moon.

Although they have been able to teleport an avatar, teleporting the inventory associated with an avatar is another story. Some inventories can include as many as 50,000 items! Do you take all you own with you when you travel? That's unheard of! You take a suitcase filled with your bare necessities when you travel. To deal with issues like this, refining Metaverse interoperability will require years of time and effort to perfect.

Imagine, in a few short years, that you will be able to access the Metaverse as easily as you do the Internet today. Interoperability is a natural progression in virtual worlds, just as the Internet advanced how we use computers. The Internet became a better tool with the addition of the browser and the refinement of the SSL. The Metaverse too will become a more useful system when it establishes a secure way to navigate from one essential place of interest to another, for business, education, or entertainment. It will be like having a virtual global positioning system (GPS) with the security of an SSL.

Working toward interoperability is not about doing more, that is, exhausting yourself with your efforts; it's about being *able* to do more with far greater efficiency and ease.

Simplifying a Complex World

When we reach the era of interoperability—a highly complex achievement—virtual worlds that meet interoperability standards will be able to interconnect. This will allow people to establish a central online identity, which they can use in compatible worlds, including private worlds. Streamlining online identity will not only simplify a complex world by maintaining one name and one reputation, it will do so by maintaining one main account for your metaversal interactions and transactions.

Imagine you are in Second Life® and decide to go to an event in another virtual world. You teleport to the event and find several members of a group that you belong to in Second Life®. They recognize you at the same time and you connect. Let's do that in reverse: You are in Second Life® and recognize the name of a person with whom you played virtual-world games. Keeping an online identity maintains your reputation throughout the Metaverse. It is also true that you may have made friends with someone years ago in one world and that someone is standing next to you at an event in another world—but neither of you know it. Many people become deeply connected with their online characters and would welcome the chance to travel the Metaverse with it.

A main identity may also centralize your online debits and credits when you make a purchase or generate a sale online. You use your bank or credit card information on the Internet to complete a transaction through an SSL, a link that is verified as secure. If you are traveling to another country, you exchange currency, perhaps using a debit card or cash for your transactions. In the metaverse, you would have your online account follow your avatar, never being without the local currency. Having a centralized account makes life, even virtual life, easier.

Private virtual worlds are a sort of gated community of the Metaverse. They are virtual worlds run on a private server, not a public one. Second Life®, for instance, is a public virtual world. Private virtual worlds are created and maintained by the developers who own or work for the private owner. What is appealing to companies is the privacy level and control. The downside (or upside, depending on your needs) is that there is no traffic in a private world. To invite clients and visitors to a private virtual world, you need them to create accounts. Gathering information on visitors to your private world may be an advantage to you, but people are adverse to creating a new account and offering their information.

Nevertheless, private worlds will also be able to become interoperable. Possibly, when the metaverse evolves, we will travel among the many private and public virtual worlds, all the while maintaining a single online identity.

Generations Online

Steve Prentice of Gartner Group believes that when virtual worlds reach the Hype Cycle plateau of productivity, then virtual worlds will last for generations. Generation I has been raised on the Internet and will find working without 3D Internet incomprehensible. In fact, they will be the ones to further develop the Metaverse and will spawn Generation M for those raised on the Metaverse. Businesses will either be prepared to meet the sophisticated needs of this maturing generation, or they will find themselves playing catchup later.

Moving Toward a Virtually Greener Pasture

At a time when individuals and large companies are making green decisions, the once misunderstood virtual world of Second Life® is being given a second look. Although it is widely popular for business and social reasons, the virtual world also holds the promise of a cleaner, greener world.

By reducing the amount of waste and pollution generated by people on the go, consumer waste can undergo a significant and immediate decrease. Virtual worlds are offering collaborative work environments in numerous ways, as described throughout the book. This is just another way of seeing the positive ways in which the future of virtual worlds looks brighter. Green decisions are made in connection with every purchase, every action, and every community and personal responsibility. Each green decision made moves you and the world farther down the right path. Include the virtual world in your green decisions.

By choice, your virtual world may consist of a few paved parking lots, but paradise is not lost. The virtual world is very forgiving that way. Virtual-world smokestacks, garbage dumps, and even litter are merely representations of the real thing, sometimes as a statement. So go ahead, pave a few parking lots (gasp), as long as they're virtual. The question about *why* you would do so in a world of infinite creative potential is left up to you to answer.

Where Do You Want to Go?

So choose your path in virtual life. Perhaps you are at the crux of a professional or life change, and you need to ask, "Where do I want to go from here?" Perhaps your business needs a fresh look, a new way to approach customers, or maybe you want to create an image with impact. You may be re-entering the workforce after a period away or just need a social outlet to keep you from going stir crazy in real life. Perhaps you have an inner child, looking to build with blocks in the sand. Do you consider yourself a social butterfly, a budding designer, a real estate tycoon, or an amusement park developer? Don't let your dreams of putting beliefs into action fade. You have the opportunity to create and reinvent how you deliver a message, live your real life, and manage your profession through the emerging virtual world.

Gartner's prediction that "eighty percent of online users will use virtual worlds by 2011" will likely come true, thus presenting the opportunity to create businesses or to redefine existing ones, promote learning, and foster personal growth. Today, virtual-world businesses are paving the way to a more efficient and technologically advanced future.

Set your personal and business GPS for the Metaverse. Your virtual vehicle has been built. The roads are paved and clear. You're the driver.

Where do you want to go?

Appendix

Second Life® Lingo Glossary

Frequently Used Acronyms and Expressions in Second Life®

afaik	far as I know
afk	away from keyboard
Alt	alternate avatar; a second (or third) avatar; like a clone, but not; people can have multiple and anonymous avatars
bf	boyfriend
brb	be right back
cya	see ya
gf	girlfriend
hb	hurry back
IM	instant message
imho	in my humble opinion; in my honest opinion
k, kk	okay
L8R	later
LL™	Linden Lab®

lmao	laughing my a** off
lmfao	laughing my f***ing a** off
lol	laughing out loud
LOL	laughing out loud (hearty laugh)
M8	mate
muah	a greeting, as in a kiss on the cheek
Newbie, Noobie, Newb	a newcomer to SL; freshman ranking
OMG	Oh, my God!
RL	real life
rotfl	rolling on the floor laughing
SL™	Second Life®
ttyl	talk to you later
ty	thank you
wb	welcome back
yvw	you're very welcome
yw	you're welcome
woot	an expression of cheer for someone or something

Index